Messages from the Universe

About the Author

Dr. Adrian Calabrese has been helping others unleash their spiritual power, achieve their greatest potential, and create miracles in their lives for the past fifteen years. She holds two doctorates, in psychical research and metaphysics, an MA in theatre/communication, and a BA in broadcasting/communications. She is a spiritual life therapist, clinical hypnotherapist, intuition consultant, teacher, medium, psychic artist, inspirational speaker, and pastor/director of the Metaphysical Center and Metaphysical Church of the Spirit.

In addition to her books, *How to Get Everything You Ever Wanted* and *10 Spiritual Steps to a Magical Life,* published by Llewellyn in both English and Spanish, Dr. Calabrese has written for *Women's World Magazine, Hysteria, New Age Retailer*, Rose Communications E-Zine, and *The Poughkeepsie Journal*. She has presented more than six hundred lectures for various groups, and is frequently interviewed on radio.

SACRED SIGNS

Hear, See & Believe Messages from the Universe

Adrian Calabrese, Ph.D.

Foreword by Richard Webster

Llewellyn Publications
Woodbury, Minnesota

First Edition
Second Printing, 2006

Book design and editing by Connie Hill
Cover image copyright © 2005 by PhotoDisc
Cover design by Kevin Brown

Llewellyn is a registered trademark of Llewellyn Worldwide, Ltd.

Library of Congress Cataloging-in-Publication Data
Calabrese, Adrian.
    Sacred signs : hear, see & believe messages from the universe /Adrian Calabrese — 1st ed.
        p.   cm.
    Includes index and bibliography.
    ISBN-13: 978-0-7387-0776-1
    ISBN-10: 0-7387-0776-7
    1. Parapsychology—Miscellanea. 2. Signs and symbols—Miscellanea. I. Title.

    BF1040.C35   2006
    133.3—dc22   2005055157

Llewellyn Publications
A Division of Llewellyn Worldwide, Ltd.
2143 Wooddale Drive, Dept. 0-7387-0776-7
Woodbury MN 55125-2989, U.S.A.
www.llewellyn.com

Printed in the United States of America

Dedicated with affection
to my dearest friend,
Loriann Burke,
whose endless compassion, caring,
generosity, support, and loving presence
are clear, unmistakable, and sacred signs
that God is truly present in my life.

Other Books by Adrian Calabrese

10 Spiritual Steps to a Magical Life

How to Get Everything You Ever Wanted

Obtenga éxito

Pasos hacia una vida magica y espiritual

Contents

Acknowledgments

As the years go by, I realize the Universe continually gives me more and more reasons to be grateful. Therefore, I am most thankful to God for all that I have and all that is yet to be, and for the opportunity to write this book. The circumstances, synchronicities, and most of all the people who have contributed to its creation and publication have blessed my life in more ways than they will ever know. It is my privilege to show my appreciation to them now.

My heartfelt thanks go first to my parents, Ann and Rudy Calabrese, for their unshakable faith in me, and for a lifetime of unconditional love, support, and guidance.

Next, I must thank the human "sacred signs" in my life, the members of the Metaphysical Center and Church of the Spirit. To my heart, they are Spirit's manifestation on earth, and never cease to amaze me with their generosity, compassion, and devotion. My soul deeply thanks: Lynn Bertrand, Janet Brady, Garth and Pamela Burger, Marcia Cavner, Sheila M. Drew, Lynn Heuermann, Nora Kiely, Billie Jane Lynch, Ondrea Lynn, Wanda Mead, Pamela and Eric Minacci, Pat O'Donnell, Karen Rapoport, Cathy Schaefer, Sara Morgan Stephenson, Alfred Szajer, Jr., Glenn Thomas, Cindy Volkert, and Jean Woods.

A book is just another idea waiting to blossom without the expertise of all the talented people who contribute to its nurturing, growth, and birth. Thank you to all the talented folks at Llewellyn Worldwide, particularly Connie Hill, my gifted editor, Kevin Brown, for his remarkable cover design, and Nancy Mostad, for believing in me and supporting this book from its conception.

Most of all, I would like to express my gratitude to Richard Webster for writing such a dynamic and complimentary foreword. What a blessing it is to have such a wonderful author contributing his positive energy to my book.

Finally, I thank all of you reading *Sacred Signs*. May you always know that the Universe stands ready to help you, now and forever.

Foreword

Over the years I've received numerous signs from the universe. I treasure these experiences as they provided hope and guidance when I needed it. They always came at difficult moments, giving me peace of mind and the assurance that everything would work out the way it should.

I have even been the source of a sign for someone else. Some years ago, I found a beautiful shell on a beach. I brought it home to give to my granddaughter. Somehow I kept forgetting to give it to her, and it sat on my desk for weeks. Finally, I decided to carry it around with me, so that I would have it when I saw her next. A few days later, my wife and I were enjoying a coffee in a café. I felt something in my pocket, and pulled out the shell. I was about to explain why I was carrying it when a lady at the next table gasped.

"That's my sign!" she exclaimed, looking at the shell. She beamed at the woman sitting with her. "I'm going to marry Tom!"

Naturally, after hearing this, I gave her the shell. I enjoyed a feeling of peace and contentment for days afterwards. It was an amazing experience to have the universe work through me in this way. It also explained why I had continually "forgotten" to give my granddaughter the shell.

Consequently, after experiences of this sort, it may seem strange that until I read Adrian Calabrese's wonderful book I never consciously asked for a sign. Even stranger is that it never occurred to me to do so. Somehow I may have thought it could only be done for matters of vital importance. Or maybe I felt I was in charge of my own life and didn't need help from the universe.

The reality, of course, is that we all need help and guidance. In *Sacred Signs*, Adrian Calabrese provides a step-by-step approach to obtaining help and confirmation at every stage of life. As a powerful bonus, this technique cannot help but increase our spiritual connection to the divine.

Since reading this book I've been using Adrian Calabrese's methods almost every day. This isn't to test the process, as I'd already experienced signs and knew they would work. It's just that the process is so satisfying, and so powerful, that I'm asking for signs all the time. This has also made me much more observant and appreciative of everything in my life.

Not long ago, I met a friend who was trapped in a career she no longer enjoyed. She was an accountant, but her dream was to grow and sell herbs. The universe had given her numerous signs that she should follow her dream, but the need for a monthly paycheck held her back and prevented her from making the change. My friend arrived at the restaurant on crutches. I was concerned, but she was blissfully happy. She had broken a leg in two places, and was having time off work to recover. She told me that the universe had forced her to have this time out to seriously think about her future. Because she had ignored all the previous signs, the universe had resorted to something more dramatic to force her to reassess her life. Over lunch she told me she'd finally decided to follow her dream. Like my friend, most of us have been given signs that we ignored for different reasons. Adrian Calabrese's three keys of asking, accepting, and trusting the universe will ensure we never do that again.

This book has the power to change lives. If you read it with an open mind, and then perform the different exercises, you'll start receiving messages from the universe. This will encourage you to experiment further, and before long you'll find yourself living a life of peace, joy, and fulfillment.

Richard Webster

Introduction

When you glanced at this book, leafed through it, decided it might be worth reading, and purchased it, you probably were not thinking that you were holding in your hand the secret to the most spectacular communication you will ever experience in your life. You were probably thinking, "It's just a book." It is much, much more. The knowledge you will gain by reading about the three keys to the knowledge of the universe will change your life forever, because you will learn to communicate directly with God. Yes, God. "Communicate with God?" you are thinking, "Where do I sign up?"

All of us have direct access to God. Whatever you wish to call the creative energy that brought forth all there is, it is waiting for you to call upon its advice, and is probably wondering what's taking you so long! God/Goddess/Spirit/Universe is a loving energy that wants you to have all that you want in this life, and is willing to help you achieve it. One of the ways in which to forge your personal communication with the Divine is by asking for guidance through what I call sacred signs.

For centuries, humankind has been asking for signs to manifest into their lives for all kinds of requests. We have always wanted to know if we should take a particular action, or avoid it like the plague! People have pleaded with God to give them some indication that their lives were on track, or that they were making the correct decision, or simply that situations would work out for them or their loved ones in a positive way. And the Universe has responded.

Spirit sends signs to us each and every day of our lives, but we are not always aware that they have arrived. Furthermore, even if we are aware that "someone" is trying to tell us "something," we usually have an extremely difficult time figuring out what that message may be. Even more frustrating for us is the inability to know what to do about a sign when it does demonstrate in our lives.

The power of the Universe is vast, yet most of us have never taken advantage of its amazing wealth of information, advice, and guidance, which when received, recognized, and understood can shape our destiny. When we live in harmony with our Source, our lives improve, and we find joy and fulfillment in each moment.

I decided to write this book because I have been the very happy recipient of divine guidance for many years. I was raised in an environment in which I was taught that I could do anything I wanted, and that there was a tremendous world of possibility out there. My Italian-American upbringing was steeped in the lore of signs, and I had no trouble believing that they were all around me, ready to "speak" to me with their cosmic wisdom.

When I was a struggling actress in New York City, I often asked God for help. "Please, get me that job!" I would cry. "I really need it! Send me a sign, God, and let me know if I will get it." Inevitably, I would perceive some indicator that that situation would work. Another actor would tell me that he "heard" I was a shoo-in for the role, a day or so after I made my plea, or I would suddenly see the last name of the director, or title of the play everywhere, in titles of books, or I would hear it in a song. At the time, I did not realize that those messages were sacred signs—the Universe trying to speak to me. I thought they were just coincidences. When they became more and more frequent, in other areas of my life as well, I started to pay attention.

I began putting together statements that included my request, and said them aloud at my prayer time. It was interesting to notice that certain wording would get a faster, more specific, detailed response, and other wording would not. My conversations with God became more and more fulfilling, and the guidance began to flow consistently and freely. Then I realized that there must be a method to working with signs, and set out to develop it. This book is the result of that quest. It worked for me and it will for you, too.

Sacred Signs is about tapping into the might of the Universe on any everyday level, to help you learn how to ask for what you need and want, and how to use that knowledge to create a better life. It is about becoming aware of receiving a response from Spirit through the appearance of signs in our daily world. It is about answered prayer. It is about carrying on a very intimate, personal, and rewarding conversation with God, each day of your life!

Within the nine chapters of *Sacred Signs* are the three important keys to the knowledge of the Universe: Ask, Accept, and Trust. The book is divided into three parts, which include easy, understandable exercises, meditations, and affirmations designed to help you to recognize and interpret your signs, and how to ask for them so that you achieve ultimate success.

Part I will give you a substantial understanding of just what sacred signs are, how you may assess your current level of spiritual knowledge, and introduces you to the keys.

Part II teaches you how to use the keys. It describes, step-by-step, how to request, recognize, interpret, and trust in your sign and its guidance. You must pay very close attention to constructing the sacred sign statements in chapter 4, because they are most important in conveying your intention to God.

Part III takes you even further into the future, and answers any other questions you might have. This final section will assist you in keeping your dialogue with Spirit going strong forever, and teaches you how to live your highest and greatest good, reaping the joys of spirit-communication by sustaining a life of peace, joy, prosperity, abundance, and physical well-being.

Enjoy the meditations and affirmations that follow in each chapter, and use them faithfully to support your sacred sign work. I have also included a sacred sign journal at the end of the book. This is a convenient place to record your work. Some of the pages have a form to use that will help in understanding the process, and the remaining pages are blank for your personal comments.

Take every opportunity to open the lines of communication with our loving Creator. When you expand your spiritual life, you increase goodness in the world, and your life becomes more joyful and fulfilling. That is what God wants for you, and he/she is waiting to tell you so. Be ready, be determined, and be patient, and all the gifts of the Universe will be given to you. Let Spirit talk to you. You will be amazed at the guidance and blessings that unfold—sign-by-sacred sign!

Part I—Turn the Key

Prepare to Unlock
the Divine Portal

Chapter One

What Is a Sacred Sign?

"It's a sign! A sign!"

With quivering hands clasped over her heart, and with a tone in her voice that was beyond question, my sainted little Italian grandmother declared that God had spoken. In my family, when God speaks, we listen. Or, at the very least, we pay attention.

My experience with these mystical messages began early, as a child growing up in the Bronx, New York. My neighborhood was a wonderful and colorful conglomeration of varied ethnicities, each with its own take on how to handle those sudden, and sometimes startling messages from the beyond. Italians, Jews, Irishmen, Germans, Puerto Ricans, African-Americans—all had a distinctive way of recognizing and interpreting these special communications.

When one grows up in the midst of this natural reliance on divine guidance, you tend to take it for granted. It wasn't until years later that I realized how very wise the personalities of my youth had been. They knew, trusted, and believed beyond the shadow of a doubt what I perceived as folklore and fairytales.

Then it happened. It was my turn to be blessed with the absolute knowledge that there existed in the Universe a power so loving and mighty that it was willing to communicate with little, insignificant me.

A penny, that's what did it—a little copper penny. I had always believed that the Universe loved and supported me, but it wasn't until that penny appeared that I knew I had found the answers to my most profound questions.

My father had been hospitalized with a series of maladies, each of which alone could have killed him. As he lay in intensive care, Mom and I stood nearby and hoped for a miracle. I was desperate to know what his fate would be.

As an intuitive therapist, I was used to receiving messages from the spirit world. I decided to make a plea to the Universe.

"A sign," I said. "Give me a sign that Dad will live."

No sooner had I said the words, than I looked down and saw a shiny new penny lying next to my left foot. It seemed to have appeared out of nowhere. I looked down several times prior to asking for my sign, and saw nothing on the floor at all. We hadn't moved an inch, so I was astonished to see the magic coin gently touching the toe of my shoe. As I picked it up, a mysterious wave of relief passed over me. Dad made it through that surgery, and nine subsequent operations, and I have ten shiny pennies to prove it!

There were other signs, too. Each time I asked, I received. I developed ways in which to ask for signs, and methods to interpret them, and taught them to my students. One by one, the stories poured in. Tangible evidence was all around that the Universe was at work, and ready to participate in our good. This, I thought, is the stuff of books.

Those who have the ability to make direct contact with the Universe intrigue us. But, what seems so mysterious is not unusual at all. Over the years, I have found a way to receive answers to all of my questions by determining exactly and specifically how to ask the God/Goddess/Spirit/Universe so that I receive a clear and indisputable answer. Of course, there are a few requirements in doing this work.

First, and foremost, a person must be willing to make the effort to ask for a sign. Second, he or she must be aware that a sign has been given, and open to and accepting of it, even if it is not what he or she wants or expects. Answers are answers, and are not always what we had in mind. Third, they must be knowledgeable as to how to recognize the sign, and interpret its message.

In this book, I have developed a sure-fire, mistake-proof method to let the Universe know what you want, and how you can successfully understand its response, so that you may live a life of joy and fulfillment through divine direction. There is no better place to go than directly to the Source. All of us can access this spiritual guidance. It is within our power and it is easier than you may think. The three keys I have developed, *Ask, Accept*, and *Trust*, are effortless to do and the results are amazing. The most difficult part of this process is contained in the last key, Trust, because it requires that you mentally and emotionally move beyond your own doubts and suspicions, and put your complete faith in the Universe. That is a daunting task for many of us.

The Nature of a Sacred Sign

Just what is a sign? It is a direct manifestation from the spirit world in material form. Tangible evidence is always present with a sign, and that is what makes it so wonderful. Finally, something we can believe in. Or do we?

It seems that we are a tough audience, we humans. We are riddled with doubt and suspicion, even when faced with undeniable evidence to the contrary. How unfortunate for us. Yet, that very element of uncertainty is what makes the impact of a sign even greater. For many of us who are die-hard realists, it takes something profound to shake us up, and make us aware that we are more than just bodies wandering the planet. When a sign appears, it restores our faith, and that is probably the most important reason that they occur.

Signs vary in nature. Some are obvious, others are not. They may come to us from loved ones who have passed on, angels, spirit guides, and of course, the big Kahuna itself—God. One of the first lovely and moving signs I remember is one that came to a client early on in my practice.

She was an older woman who had just lost her husband. As was to be expected, she was grieving and having a very difficult time coping with his loss. She was devastated by the loneliness she felt each day, and wanted to know if her dear husband was aware of her feelings. In a session, she asked me to contact him and inquire. I did so, and he responded that he was aware of her feelings. Intuitively, I sensed that she needed further convincing. I suggested she ask him herself. This was a concept that startled her.

"Will he hear me?" she asked.

"Yes. He heard me, didn't he? Why don't you give it a try?" I responded.

"How?" She was intrigued.

"Just ask him for a sign," I said.

I hadn't seen her for several weeks. In her next session, she said she wanted to show me a very special sympathy card she had received from a friend. It was distinctive because it had been several years since her husband died, and its arrival was unexpected. The friend who sent it had just found out about his passing within the last few weeks. I looked at the card, and was struck by the beautiful rose painted on the cover. Inside was a poem about the flower, and how it was a symbol of eternal love. The card went on to say that such love remains in our hearts even after we leave the Earth.

"The card is from my husband," she said with conviction. "I asked him to send me a rose, to let me know that he's still with me, and hears me when I speak to him. It's my favorite flower, and he gave them to me all the time."

Signs can come in the strangest of ways, and in many forms. My client was wise enough to realize that a rose is a rose is a rose. Any one of us might have expected a real living rose to appear, and sometimes they do, but in this case, the rose was just part of the sign. The message in the poem was even more important.

So, you see, whether it is roses or pennies, signs appear in the most synchronistic of circumstances, when you least expect them, or when you do. The trick is in knowing when they have made their way into your life, and then not censoring them if they come in a form that is unexpected.

Signs can be comforting, startling, interesting, or unusual. They can come in common ways, delivered directly to us from Spirit. Before I began my spiritual work, I came face-to-face with a most profound and sacred sign.

While shopping in a bookstore, I felt it my duty as a caring consumer to place a book back on the shelf that had been lying on its back atop the others. As I filed it away, the title caught my attention. It was a book called *Spirit Guides*, by Iris Belhayes and Enid, her guide. I was a novice to the concept of guides, but felt compelled to buy the book. That very night, I heard the voice of my own guide, Roger, for the first time. Coincidence? I think not. From that moment, my life changed forever.

I could go on citing other examples of these miraculous messages, and I will include many in the course of this book. Simple or profound, this tangible evidence is ready to make its way into your life, and probably already has.

Where Do Signs Come From?

Practically speaking, there really is no mystery to the manifestation of signs. Nothing is impossible for God. Materializing and dematerializing matter is a small task for Spirit. I learned this lesson as a teenager. Growing up Catholic, I was perplexed by the notion of the virgin birth, one of the more startling tenets of the religion for a teenage girl. I posed my question to my favorite priest, Father Flynn. With childlike wonder I asked, "How could the Virgin Mary give birth, and still be a virgin?" It just did not compute in my head. He looked me straight in the eye, and with absolute conviction said, "Don't you believe God can do anything? The Immaculate Conception is no sweat for Him."

That did it for me. I haven't forgotten that conversation, because it was at that precise moment I realized the power of God. If the Immaculate Conception is "no sweat," signs are definitely small potatoes! Of course, you have to believe in God to accept that. But, even if you are not a believer, you are still going to receive your signs. That is the beauty and benevolence of the Universe.

Metaphysicians believe that what we send into the Universe we receive back. It's called the Universal Law of Circulation, or Reciprocity. In other words, what you give, you get. In terms of signs, that means that when you make a request with a sincere intention, you will receive a response which will keep you sincere. God will answer your request, so you will continue to send that loving, trusting message. God wants you to be happy and to have this guidance. Where is it written that we're supposed to go through life wondering about everything? The loving, benevolent God I know wants to help me live my best life and is willing to guide me to it. What better way than through outright, direct communication? I cannot think of any. Start talking to your God, because you deserve to be happy.

Signs can come from several sources. They may come directly from the Universe, or through people who have passed on, spirit guides, or angels. They will most often appear in your material world as a physical manifestation. Sometimes signs will come to you through folks living here on the Earth with us. Yes, even you might be a messenger delivering a sign, as was the friend who sent the card to my grieving client. If you have been selected by the Universe to do its bidding, chances are you will not realize it. You will just feel motivated to do something loving for someone else out of the goodness of your heart, and boom, you're an instant messenger! Since it is obvious that, at times, God needs us to execute his/her plan, it would behoove us to be willing stewards. You never know whose angel you will be!

Warning Signs

There are times when a sign will come to us to warn us of an upcoming event that may have a great impact on our lives. When a sign comes as a warning you might not recognize it until its results have manifested in your life. This happens because the spiritual seeker does not know how to recognize or interpret the sign. Do not worry. By the end of this book, you will be able to spot even the most complicated warning signs. When a warning sign appears, it may portend a potentially upsetting or frightening event; therefore, it is often ignored or denied. We should not live each day worrying about what scary signs will pop into our world. However, it is important to be aware that when a sign appears that seems negative, it is probably trying to tell you to pay closer attention to what is happening around you. To ease your mind, please realize that a warning sign is just that—a warning. Realistically speaking, sometimes signs do warn us of difficult situations that are imminent, but they are not necessarily predictions of doom. Rather, a sign may be an attempt by the Universe to alert you that you will soon have to make changes in your life. Not all warning signs are frightening. Some show up to tell us to be careful driving, or to wear a sweater so we will not catch cold. Stay calm when one appears in your life.

In my life, I have received several warning signs. The most recent was astounding. Two years ago, I was at home in my office, hard at work writing my second book, when I heard a strange noise downstairs. It sounded like a flapping noise inside a hollow can. It would begin and go on for a few seconds, stop, and then start again, but only for a few short bursts. The sound persisted. I followed it to my living room to the wood-burning stove. That fluttering sound was scaring me, and I jumped each time I heard it. It just wouldn't stop. I soon realized that something was trapped in the stove. After a few more moments, it began to chirp. A little bird had fallen in through the chimney. I thought that strange, since it had a cap on it and a grid, but nonetheless, a bird had gotten in.

I must confess, I am a little afraid of birds, but I was upset that this poor little thing was stuck in there, yet I was too afraid to let it out. My partner at the time was a "nature boy," as I liked to call him, and was very good and gentle with all animals. I immediately sent out the alarm. He came over, opened the stove door, gently cupped the poor thing in his hands, and set it free outside. I thought it was an odd occurrence. Little did I know that this adventure was a sign, and a profound one at that.

That was a Monday. On Wednesday night I returned home after a wonderful evening get-together with friends, to see my beautiful townhouse ablaze. The unit next to mine had caught fire and spread to my home. As I drove into the complex there were fire engines everywhere, and I remember saying, "Oh my God, I wonder whose home it is. I hope it's not mine." It was.

I realized days later that "the bird-in-the-stove" was a clear and unmistakable sign that something to do with fire was about to affect my life. That little bird was a symbol of me. I was the bird in the stove! The bird was freed unharmed, as was I. I was not even home when the fire happened. That, in itself, was unusual. I am home most weeknights. I realized that the Universe was trying to tell me that whatever happened concerning fire, I would be safe, using the plight of that little bird as the messenger. I thanked and blessed that bird. Each time one appears in my life, I take heed.

So, you see, warning signs can also let us know that we will be okay, even though we might have to make a few unexpected adjustments to our lives.

Unexpected Signs

Earlier, I mentioned that you have most likely received signs throughout your life but did not realize it or recognize them. You do not always have to ask for a sign to be the recipient of one. These unexpected signs are the ones that occur without our direct intervention or request. The "bird-in-the-stove" was such a sign. God knows when we need reassurance or confirmation about certain issues or problems in our lives, and chooses to communicate with us through a spontaneous expression like a sign, to let us know that our prayers are being heard, and that we are not alone. Unexpected signs let us know that help is on the way from the Universe, even if we haven't asked for it!

I am a member of a prestigious authors' organization that holds a yearly conference. It is very well attended by hundreds of authors and journalists. This year, I was a new member. All the new members had a blue ribbon attached to their name badge so that current members could easily identify them. Current members would welcome the new members into the fold, and make them feel comfortable. It is a lovely gesture. I looked forward to being a member and wearing my blue ribbon, but I had doubts as to whether or not I would be a good fit for this noble group. I went to the conference wondering if I had what it takes to be numbered among these noble professionals.

When I went over to the welcome table, much to my surprise, they had no record of my registration or membership. Luckily, I had a copy of it with me. They apologized and gave me a handwritten badge, with no ribbon.

"Okay. I'll get over it," I thought. "It's only a ribbon."

I was beginning to feel that the badge mix-up was a sign that I really didn't belong among this elite. The day went on, no one welcomed me, and I felt sadder and sadder about the message that I thought was coming through from the Universe. I was looking forward to lunch to network and meet some people, and decided to put my insecurities aside. My tablemates introduced themselves, and when they heard I was a new member, took care of the welcoming and comforting for me. A distinguished line of authors spoke at the luncheon, and all I could dream about was someday being numbered among them.

"Do I really belong here?" I thought.

After the last speaker was through, the president of the organization walked to the podium and said, "I have one last announcement that just must be done before we end. Adrian Calabrese, are you in the room?"

For a moment there I forgot my own name. I was stunned. Among five hundred people, I shyly raised my hand.

"We need to apologize to you, Adrian," he said. "We found your membership and your new member badge, and we're so sorry for the mix-up. Please come up and get it."

I stumbled to the podium and gratefully claimed my badge with the blue ribbon. The fact that this group of professionals was respectful enough to make sure I was taken care of, convinced me that this is where I belong, and where I definitely want to be. I guess God thought I needed major convincing to stifle my doubts and insecurities! Everyone in the place knew who I was that day, a respected colleague.

Now that is some unexpected sign, don't you think? Can you identify a similar event in your life, when you were given an answer even before you asked the question? Did it seem that a sign magically appeared as a response to your mere thoughts? I'm sure you can. Amazing, isn't it?

When Is a Sign Not a Sign?

At this stage, I realize that you are just trying to understand this mystical manipulation, and how these messages appear in your physical world. There are times when you think you have done all the right things, had the most loving intention, and said the appropriate words, but, to your knowledge, your sign does not appear. Sometimes we must wait for our signs, but they always come, even if they do not seem to.

It is important to your growth to accept the fact that not receiving a sign *is* a sign. There is never a time when you ask for a sign and do not get one. So, when is a sign, not a sign? Never. Get it? Good. That means you accept the concept that there is also a "yes/no" aspect to the Universe, the cosmic yin/yang. Whether or not you receive a material sign depends upon how you ask for it. But, whether your sign materializes or not, you will get an answer. If it does not manifest in a concrete form, the sign is either "no," or it is still forthcoming. Signs and their appearance, or lack thereof, are still powerful messages.

What About Timing?

This brings us to another, sometimes touchy, issue—timing. It is important not to feel as though you have not received an answer to your question if the sign does not appear immediately in your world. It might take longer for some signs to manifest, depending upon what you asked for.

I once read an article written by an author who wrote a book about Superman, and was having no luck selling it to a publisher. He asked for a sign that he should continue to pursue publication. In a few days, when no sign seemed to appear, he gave up on the hope that he would receive one. Months later, while walking along a beach, he was contemplating his unpublished manuscript and the trouble he was having. He stopped for a moment to enjoy the tranquility of the sea. As he playfully dug his foot into the sand, he felt something beneath it. He bent down to explore further and reached into the sand. What he discovered astounded him. It was a toy replica of Superman, red cape and all! What are the odds? Astronomical. Of course, he believed this to be a sign that he should continue to pursue the publication of his book. It took a few months for the sign to appear, but it was well worth the wait.

Signs may appear in minutes, hours, days, weeks, months, or even years! This, my friends, is out of our hands. God knows the right and perfect time for us to receive our sign, better than we do, and such mysteries remain inexplicable. But, the good news is that in all my years of asking for signs, they have never taken more than hours or days to appear.

Alternately, we may choose to impose time constraints ourselves in the way we request the sign. We can be very specific about timing, if we choose. I will go into detail about how to ask for your signs in chapter 4, but for now, take a look at this example.

Let's say you want to know if you will marry Harry. You could simply ask for a sign confirming that, and wait and see what you get. Or, you might rephrase the request and send a different message to the Universe. You could say that if you don't receive a sign within a specific time period, say twenty-four hours, that you will assume the answer to your question is "no." This method is definitely not for the faint of heart, but it is extremely effective.

Multiple Signs

There may be occasions when you will ask for one sign and receive several. When this occurs, it is quite convincing. We cannot ever know how many signs we will receive when we request spiritual intervention. Perhaps Spirit knows that you are difficult to persuade, and that it just takes more evidence for you to take serious action. Or, the answer is so important that multiple signs come to demonstrate how very important the issue is, and to get you moving on it!

Recently, I asked for a penny again, my sign of choice. Whenever I am blue or uncertain about which way to go in a situation, I ask for a penny to appear to let me know that everything is going to work out okay, no matter what action I take or decision I make. I was toying with the notion of hiring a personal publicist. Publicists cost lots of money, but if you want folks to hear your message, you need to get it out there. I have no expertise in that area, so hiring someone who does made sense. I believe that God is the source of my prosperity, so I knew I would find the money somehow. That wasn't the issue. There are hundreds of competent publicists out there. The issue was: who would be best for me? After narrowing down the field to a hundred and fifty or so, and then finally to seven, I began to interview them. When I was down to three, I favored one, and asked God for my sign that she would be the right choice.

Shortly after asking, I left my office to return home. It was raining like crazy, but as I made the mad dash to my car, I stepped on—you guessed it—a penny! Wait, it doesn't stop there. It was so wet, I didn't pick it up, but I knew that was my sign and kept going, joyful in the knowledge that the Universe had responded within minutes. When I got home, I opened the car door to exit. There on the ground was another one! The next day, as I strolled through my favorite store, I found another. Needless to say, I now have the right and perfect publicist for me, special delivery from the Universe.

When multiple signs appear, take heed. They mean business, and their sense of urgency is impressive.

Sign Abuse

I feel compelled to talk about another sensitive subject I call, "sign abuse." Yes, there are those sacred sign junkies among us who, once they have mastered the art of spirit communication, get crazy and constantly request them. There really is no danger in this action. What is dangerous is what is going on in the sign junkie's mind. They drive themselves nuts looking for signs everywhere, or, what's worse, make excuses for their behavior using the signs as a crutch for not taking responsibility for their actions. If you undertake to work with your Creator using signs as your primary tool of divine expression, you must do so with restraint, integrity, and wise judgment. All spiritual undertakings must be approached in this way. As you read along, you'll discover how to keep your perspective about this work, and how to be both objective and fair in your assessment of sacred signs.

Another drawback of sign abuse is scattered energy. This can do more damage to your spiritual work than anything else. Think about it. If you have too many things to do at once, you become overloaded. I don't know anybody who isn't on overload at one time or another. Spiritual overload may delay or prevent your sacred signs from appearing when you:

- ask for more than one sign at once, and

- doubt that you will actually receive one.

It is easy to get excited about signs. I know. I was so excited I wrote this book!

But *focus* is the important thing here. You will need to prioritize in order to be effective. Most of us are pretty weak when it comes to chatting with the Universe. We get flabbergasted easily. When you begin to receive your signs, you might treat it as I do, like a bowl of potato chips, and just one is never enough! Therein lies the problem. Decide what is most pressing in your life, at the moment, and ask for just one sign to assist with that situation. When you have received the sign, then, and only then, may you move on to the next request. If you make too many requests at once, you will send a message to the Universe that you are confused, and guess what? That is what you will get back. Pace yourself, do not scatter your energy, and you will get better results.

Preparatory Exercises

As is true of all spiritual efforts, the seeker must always prepare for the experience. We learn best when we focus our mind and concentrate on the issue at hand. I have created the following exercises to help you focus your energy and prepare you for sacred sign work. They will help you to assess your current receptivity to the appearance of signs in your life. Give this first exercise a try. I assure you, you will find out some pretty important information about how you view life, and that realization alone is worth the effort!

Exercise #1

Try to answer these questions objectively. This is not a test, and no one is grading you so be as honest with yourself as possible. For future reference, you may record your answers here or on the blank pages in the Sacred Sign Journal included at the back of this book.

1. Do you believe that life exists beyond the physical world? Why or why not?

yes, I know that once we pass, our souls are still here & never die

2. Do you believe that we can communicate with spirits, entities, or God? Why or why not?

yes, I can sometimes feel my mom, my late husband, Grandma & uncle Richard

3. Are you a skeptic or a believer in synchronicity, the concept that seemingly random events occur in a right and perfect order in our lives in direct response to our needs as we communicate them to the Universe?

completely believe in synchronicity, there are no accidents

4. Are you willing to do all it takes to communicate your needs to the Universe, and be receptive to its response?

without a doubt!

Let's take a look at your answers. Question #1 asks you to confront your fears. It might not be obvious at first, but when the subject of life beyond this Earth comes up, it scares many of us. People who have willingly come to a session with me have actually sat shaking with fear, even though they have initiated the visit and want information from Spirit. If the thought of communicating with God incites fear in you, you might not be ready to ask for signs. Your fear could block your receptivity to them. But, on the other hand, if your answer to this question is a confident "yes," you are the perfect candidate.

Chances are that if you answered the first question with a negative response, it will be echoed in question #2. If you don't believe that life exists beyond this planet, then you can't possibly believe we can communicate with it, right? Right. But, if you do believe that life exists on other planes, then it is logical to you that we can communicate with it. Correct? Yes, we can.

Question #3 draws your attention to the concept of synchronicity coined by the respected psychologist, Carl Jung. If you see all things as random and coincidental, then you are not ready to do sign work. If you see the Universe as planned and deliberate, you're ready to go!

Finally, question #4 asks for a commitment. If you are not willing to do all it takes to ask for a sign and all it takes to understand it, then you will not get the clear answers you deserve, because your doubt will scatter your energy and you'll send a message to the Universe that is not focused or confident. And, as you know, you will receive what you send.

Exercise #2

The following questions are designed to help you assess your powers of observation, an extremely necessary skill in interpreting sacred signs. Years ago I taught acting technique and used similar questions. The actor's craft depends upon being a skilled observer of life. Here is your chance to see if you have star potential!

Record your answers as you did with the first exercise.

1. When you are introduced to someone for the first time, do you tend to remember his or her name?

yes, very much so, I always call people by their first name!

2. Would you remember his or her eye color, even if it were not distinctive in any way?

yes, I always look a person over + scan their entire body

3. Observe the palm of your dominant hand. Tomorrow, observe it again and see if you notice any changes in the configuration of lines and creases.

right hand strong, veiny

4. What do you notice about the sound of someone's voice? Think of a friend or loved one, and try to describe their voice in a sentence or two.

Jenny, very mexican accent
Roxanne, very crisp + decesive
dez, very nurturing & intellgt

5. Are you able to decipher what someone is "not" saying by the expression on their face?

yes, sometimes I almost feel I can read minds

I hope that after doing this exercise you realize how important it is to be sensitive to your environment and aware of its nuances. There are no right or wrong answers. If you found that your responses to the questions came easily and quickly, you are probably a very observant person. If you had to think awhile, you'll need to work on paying closer attention to the world around you, so that you'll be better able to discern your sacred signs when they come your way.

Prepare to Tap into the Power: Meditation

If all that I have said makes sense to you, you are ready to tackle the challenge of communicating with the Universe. Yes, it is a challenge, and like any other challenge, it requires dedication and above all, knowledge. To prepare to work with Sacred Signs, you must make your instrument, your mind, calm and receptive to the messages. The best way I know to do that is through meditation. I am not talking about anything seriously intense here. Meditation is a simple way for you to eliminate the stresses of life for a few moments, and allow your mind to experience peace. This one is designed to get you used to relaxing and opening to your spiritual self.

Relaxation Meditation

Find a comfortable position in your chair, hands on your lap, and feet flat on the floor. Close your eyes, take three gentle breaths, inhaling through the nose, and exhaling through the mouth. Continue breathing gently with mouth closed. As you do, focus your mind on the top of your head, and begin to allow a wave of relaxation to move down your body slowly. . . . Guide the feeling of relaxation to move down your neck, very, very slowly, over your shoulders . . . down your arms, and out through your finger tips. . . . Now focus your mind on moving the feeling of relaxation down your torso . . . your chest . . . down the back to the lower back . . . down over the waist . . . the hips . . . down the legs . . . over the ankles . . . and over the tops of the feet. . . . Finally, feel a gentle tingle in the soles of your feet and imagine the wave of relaxation flowing through you like a gentle breeze, out the soles of your feet into the ground below. Just relax in that moment for a bit. . . . When you are ready and fully relaxed, take another gentle breath, and as you exhale, open your eyes.

That is all there is to it, to chill out for a moment. This meditation is good at any time you need it, not just for sacred sign purposes. Use it when you feel most stressed, to take the edge off your day or a difficult emotional event. Each chapter will include a meditation to assist you in manifesting your sign.

Now you have learned to quiet those noisy thoughts and find peace, even if only for a moment. It is important to clear your mind and calm down, to open the door to images and impressions from your higher mind, your soul, your spirit, and God. That's all it takes, just a simple moment of tranquility to contact the most amazing force in the Universe.

Prepare to Tap into the Power: Affirmation

There is just one more thing you need to do before we move on to the next phase of preparing to ask the cosmos for your sign. As a minister and metaphysician, I always use affirmations to pave the way to every spiritual activity I undertake. Affirmations are carefully worded statements directed to God/Spirit and in some religious circles (mine for instance) considered prayer. Anyone can use them to set forth a positive intention, and that is what we will use them for when asking for our sacred signs. Each chapter will include an affirmation to assist you in your sign work. The following is a preparatory affirmation to open your spiritual center to receiving messages from the Universe.

Preparatory Affirmation

Thank you, God/Goddess/Spirit, for calming my mind and heart, and opening my spiritual channels to receive your messages. I am willing to release any blocks and outmoded or fearful thoughts about communicating with you, and ask that you guide me to my highest good. And so it is!

Now that you have taken a look at your feelings about direct communication with Spirit, calmed your mind with a simple meditation, and affirmed your intention to prepare to receive your good, you are ready to move forward.

Helpful Hints for Sign Seekers

Now here's a startling revelation for you: sacred signs will come to you whether you do all of this or not. Yes, it sounds as though I'm shooting holes into my own system, but I have learned over the years that all it takes to contact otherworldly energy is a loving heart and honorable intention. Many signs have already come your way in your lifetime, but you have not recognized them. Your mind is the greatest tool you possess. What you think, is what you get. Focus your mind on a single idea and you can work miracles! Signs are just the tangible manifestation of focused thought. It is time to look more deeply into what you need and what you want, so that you can form a strong and effective intention, and invite divine assistance into your life.

To further assist you, I have included an "Important Points" summary at the end of each chapter. It will help you organize your thoughts and remember the process so that your sign work will be most effective.

Important Points to Remember

- You must be willing to make the effort to ask for a sign.

- You must be aware that a sign has been given, and open to and accepting of it.

- You must be knowledgeable as to how to recognize the sign and interpret its message.

- A sign is a direct manifestation from the spirit world in material form.

- Signs vary in nature.

- Signs can come in common ways and forms.

- Even if you are not a believer, you will receive signs.

- Signs can come from the Universe, souls in spirit, angels, spirit guides, and through living persons.

- Sometimes we must wait for signs, but they always come.

- Not receiving a sign *is* a sign.

- You may request particular timing for a sign.

- You may receive multiple signs.

- Multiple signs demonstrate the importance of an issue.

- When multiple signs appear, take heed.

- Prepare to tap into your spiritual power through meditation.

- Prepare to tap into your spiritual power through affirmation.

- Sacred Signs may come to you whether you make an effort to receive them or not.

- Your thoughts are the greatest and most powerful tools you possess.

Chapter Two

Soul Searching

Brave soul that you are, you have continued to read and I assume, have made a decision to try this sign thing for yourself. Wonderful. But, and there's always a "but," you will need to take some time to analyze your own past history concerning signs. Before you can get really good at asking for and receiving sacred messages from the Universe, you need to take a close look at your past, and discover the signs that you have already received in your lifetime. There will be exercises in this chapter to help you do that, but for now, let's talk a bit about you.

First of all, it takes confidence to do this sign work. Are you a person who is intrigued by supernatural phenomena, or are you someone who thinks it is all hype? It really does not matter if you are willing and open to trying something new. The truth is, believer or not, everyone has been the recipient of a sacred sign at some point in their lives. Whether or not you have seen it as such depends upon your spiritual path.

In the nineteenth century, sociologist Carl Jung coined the term, "synchronicity." It is loosely defined as the unfolding of events in our lives in an orderly and systematic fashion, usually to a good end. Many have called this series of fortuitous events a coincidence. Synchronicities are more than just coincidences. They are planned, carefully engineered occurrences that fall into a right and perfect spiritual order, and sometimes have deep impact on our lives. Synchronicity is not random. Neither is the Universe. And, believe it or not, neither are the events of your life.

What most of us do not understand is that we have a measure of control over the appearance of synchronicities in our world. Our will alone is capable of invoking such energy. In other words, if we want something badly enough, our sheer determination will send an unseen, silent message into the Universe that will actually cause outward events to occur in our lives. Then synchronicity kicks in and everything seems to "fall into place" surrounding the need or desire upon which we are placing our focus.

For instance, suppose you are seeking a new job. For whatever reason, you feel the need to seek out a new work situation. Since work is so important to so many of us, it is safe to say that this would be a high priority in your life. Therefore, you are probably focusing a lot of your thought energy on it. You are probably experiencing sleepless nights, spending hours contemplating where to look, or how to look, whom to call, etc., until you come up with a plan of action. All of that think-tank stuff generates spiritual energy and becomes focused thought. Energy does not dissipate. It has to exist somewhere. In this instance, it flies straight to the Universe as what is known in metaphysical circles as "intention."

Intention is powerful because it acts like a bullet to a target. In this case, the target is God/Spirit. When your message or intention in the form of focused thought is perceived by the Universe, your answer is forthcoming. In order for the answer to reach you in your physical world, Spirit uses the tools at hand, events, happenings, and people, to deliver the message. These circumstances unfold in a right and perfect order and the process of manifesting begins. It might go something like this:

You mention to a friend that you're looking for a new place to work. Your friend says "it just so happens" that he knows a guy, who knows a guy, who has a job opening and would probably love to have someone like you work for him. He gives you the telephone number, and you call and get an interview without a problem or wait. The interviewer loves you, and it goes so well, you can't believe it. Your second interview is better than the first, and within two weeks, voila! You get a new job. What a coincidence, you think, but no, it is synchronicity at work.

Synchronicity is an integral part of the process when you ask for sacred signs. It is the method the Universe uses to get the answer to you. It is your responsibility to pay close attention, and register the "coincidental" happenings that begin to occur in your life. When they do, you will see an understandable pattern, and eventually you will interpret it as your sign.

What About Luck?

Synchronicity is not coincidence, nor is it luck. Luck has nothing at all to do with manifesting the signs you have requested. It wasn't luck that I looked down and found my pennies, any more than it was luck that you got your new job. Everything in life, although it seems random and out of our control, is not. When you work with spiritual energy and unseen power, you can change your world. Signs let you know that your handiwork is successful. On the contrary, luck implies that things are out of your control and magically come together through sheer happenstance. It infers that we have nothing to do with the development of our good, and how it comes to us. Luck doesn't require effort. We just need to hang out and wait for it to happen. The truth is that luck just doesn't happen. It is a result of efforts put forth by intention and will.

For instance, you go to Las Vegas, thinking, "I'm going to get lucky at the crap tables this time!" Guess what? That's an intention to win. You are sending the message to the Universe that you have the will to win, unless of course, you're just hoping to win. Winning requires confidence, i.e. focused thought. People win because they expect to, not by chance. I know that this is a difficult concept to grasp, but that is the principle behind achievement of any kind. Somewhere in your psyche, you must believe beyond the shadow of a doubt that you can win. Then you do. Luck has nothing to do with it. I know someone who never loses each time she goes gambling. She has this great attitude that she will win. She approaches the day with joy and confidence, and she always wins. It is not luck. It is focused thought. Period.

Luck is not a spiritual concept. It is a secular one. If you live your life waiting for luck to strike, you might wait a very, very long time. If you live with confidence, intention and focus, you won't wait long for good things to happen. Sacred signs do not depend on luck. They depend on directed effort, spiritual fortitude, and trust. Get those three going for you and you'll be unstoppable!

Negative Signs: Signs You Don't Really Want to See

At this point, I must tell you that there will be times when a sign appears that you really do not want. You might have all the hope and promise in the world that something will work out for you, or is right for you, and the last thing you want is a sign from the Universe that you're moving in the wrong direction, or that what you want is probably not good for you. It has happened to all of us. Doors slam in our faces, people leave us, relationships break up, we lose jobs, and go through trauma of all kinds. We tend to ignore the obvious if we want something badly enough, and discount the signs that all is not developing the way we'd like it to. In soul searching, you must come face-to-face with this sort of intrapersonal deception.

One of these unwanted signs arrived for me through yet another bird. It was apparent to me that had I paid attention to that "bird-in-the-stove," I might not have been as shocked as I was when the actual fire happened in my townhouse. Since that time, I've paid extra close attention to my signs, particularly to birds.

One fall morning, while I was living in temporary housing after the fire, I was awakened very early, at about six o'clock, to a rapping sound. It was coming from the main floor of the house, and it was so loud I heard it up on the second floor where the bedrooms were located. Of course, being the chicken that I am, I picked up a heavy object, and slowly crept down the stairs, all the time focusing my keenest attention on the very sharp sound beckoning me forward. As I gingerly got to the bottom of the very steep staircase, I could tell the sound was coming from the left side of the main floor, toward the sliding glass doors that led to the backyard. As I approached them, I could not believe my eyes. A very large bird was launching kamikaze attacks on the sliding glass doors, and thrusting itself, beak first, into them, wings, feathers, and talons flying madly! As I watched in disbelief, the bird hit the window with such deliberate force, it knocked itself out, fell to the ground, and

God bless it, rallied, picked itself up, and took off into the sky. To my shock, he flew a loop no airline pilot could duplicate, and proceeded to make another beeline for the same spot on the window! He did this repeatedly, for two hours.

Needless to say, I tried everything I could to scare that bird away. I blocked the window with blankets, thinking that it was mistaking its own reflection for another intrusive bird, and attacking it. I had heard that playing music might calm a bird, so I piped out some soothing New Age tunes through an adjoining window. You should have seen me as I jumped up and down in front of it, shooing it, and looking quite the fool, but all to no avail. This dance might have gone on all day, for all I know. I had to get out of the house after two hours, because I couldn't take it any-more. When I arrived home that evening, there was only the remaining vestige of lost feathers, but no bird in sight. It never returned, but something else did.

The next night, I realized what the bird was telling me. At about three in the morning, I was awakened again, to the pitter patter of little feet running in the attic above my bed. It sounded as though there were about two hundred mice, or squir-rels, or whatever it is that runs in attics. It was so terrifying and spine-tingling, I frantically phoned my landlord screaming, "Please do something, now!" The exter-minator arrived and discovered a "family" of twenty or thirty mice building their nests and playing games up there. They were eating holes in the ceiling, and he said that because there were so many of them, they might have eventually fallen through and landed on my bed! Ugh! It took three months to catch them all.

At this point, you're wondering what the bird was telling me, right? I determined that it was alerting me to the possibility of imminent trouble that was potentially more harmful to me than the bird's own activities. The Universe was not telling me what that trouble was specifically, but I was being given a cosmic wake-up call to stay alert in my world, because an uncomfortable circumstance was at bay. Spirit uses animals to carry messages to us, and the dear ones generously offer their assis-tance, often at the expense of their own lives. I interpreted the sign as a negative one, because the action of the bird was so potentially harmful to itself, to the house, and to me for that matter. I knew from past experience that when an animal-sign is in trouble, something will go wrong.

The problem with negative signs is that we don't always know what the sign is trying to tell us or what the resulting circumstance will be. The reason for our not knowing is that God often supplies guiding information to us to facilitate the lessons we have undertaken to learn in this lifetime, without spoiling the fun of learning them. Sometimes, I wish the Universe would just mess with my free will, and tell me what's going to happen! But, alas, the Divine doesn't work that way. Divine intervention occurs when we are not meant to be harmed, but have put ourselves into a position that is compromising our well-being. The Universe sometimes helps keep our suffering to a minimum by warning us of impending difficulties.

I am sure you can recall a sign in your life that implied a difficult event was on the way. When an outrageous, negative, or simply unusual circumstance occurs that makes you think, "I wonder why that happened," my advice is to prepare yourself by tuning into what is happening in your immediate environment. You will be very glad you did.

Stop Signs

Signs offer us two options in life, either to move forward with our chosen activities, or to put a halt to them. "Stop Signs" are those that are clear indicators that we should consider not doing what we have planned to do. They require trust, because we do not usually know why we keep running into obstacles on our path, and our human tendency is to plow ahead in spite of them. But, there are some obstacles that are deliberately thrown our way, to ensure that we reconsider our original intention. For example, consider the following scenario.

On a bright, sunny summer afternoon, you might decide to take a nice long, relaxing drive in the country. You set out to leave, but you can't find your keys. Thirty minutes later after a frantic search, keys in hand, you finally set out on your way. You get into your car, and you see you have no gas. When you arrive at the gas station, the pump eats your credit card. "Okay," you think, "it'll be fine. I'll call the station tomorrow and get it handled," and you proceed on your way. You get three or four miles out of town, when you discover you have a flat tire. You find yourself saying, "Boy, something is trying to tell me something. Maybe I shouldn't be going on this drive after all." Guess what? You're right. It is at this point that you need to pay attention to the circumstances around you, your gut, and what it's telling you, and not your desires. When so many things go wrong it is a red flag moment that you must heed. It is the Universe telling you not to proceed, to stop. Stop signs are not usually welcomed, but they are another way that Spirit communicates our highest good to us. We will often not know why we are being advised to stop. We may never know, or we may hear of a terrible accident in the news that occurred on the very road we were about to take on that drive in the country. Ask yourself how many times you have ignored the stop signs, and ended up regretting it. Stop signs tell us to think twice. They can sometimes even save our lives.

Go Signs

Just as stop signs may get in the way of a good time, "Go Signs" encourage us to have one. They help us make decisions, indicate that we should proceed with an action, or notify us that we are on the right track in our efforts. My lovely assistant and dear friend, Ondrea, told me of just such a decision-making experience.

It seems she was about to paint the interior of her home, a chore that many of us have undertaken. But, when you are a keen seeker of spiritual guidance, such a mundane task takes on greater significance. She was undecided as to which brand of paint she should purchase. Standing in the paint store parking lot, she pondered over a decision between Sherwin-Williams or Behr, and wanted to be sure before entering the store to avoid confusion. Therefore, Ondrea, being the good and faithful soul searcher she is, asked for a sign as to which to choose. Seconds after asking, a large tractor-trailer driving along the main road caught her eye. Painted on its side, in clear and unmistakable view, was the word, "Behr." Which one do you think she purchased?

As odd as it seems, the Universe wants to help us with even the simplest of decisions. Go signs help us to live a peaceful, struggle-free life of joy and abundance in direct contact with Spirit. The Universe does not judge the magnitude of our tasks, and therefore, no job is a small or insignificant one in the eyes of God. Go signs are available to us for all the choices we need to make, small or significant.

Go signs also answer "yes/no" questions we may have concerning whether to proceed with a plan or not. Ondrea had a great example of this one, too.

My assistant told me that years ago she asked for a sign telling her whether to accept a particular job. At the time she was a struggling actress in New York and needed a "day job" to pay the rent. She was offered several, but one at a very famous, upscale restaurant was most attractive to her. Since she had no experience in the field, she was unsure that it would be a good fit, and decided to ask Spirit for help. She asked for a rose in some form to be shown to her as a sign that the answer was "yes." The next day as she was driving in her car, the radio played a comical commercial that consisted of dialogue between two voices. She knew she had gotten her answer when she clearly heard the line, "You win a rose." That did it. She took the job and worked there happily for almost four years. It turned out to be the perfect job, providing her with the money to rent a room in New York City, and ample opportunity to go to auditions to pursue her acting career.

Go signs may indicate that we are on the right track with our efforts, as well. If Ondrea doesn't mind, I have one of these to tell you about. Recently, I have been putting effort into pursuing inspirational speaking opportunities around the country. I have been speaking and lecturing for thirty years, but have not pursued it on a national professional level, and therefore, I had my doubts. All the insecurities flare up when we make these important decisions, and they sometimes cloud our better judgment. In this case, going forward means spending a sizable amount of money on speaker kits, travel expenses, publicity, etc., and I am always cautious when I make this type of investment. It is always my practice to ask God for help in making important decisions, and so I did. I asked that I receive a sign that I should continue to pursue speaking opportunities, and I added that I would accept any form in which it would manifest to me. In three short days, I got my answer—twice.

Three days after asking for my go sign, I had the privilege of being a guest on a radio show broadcast from Maine. The host doing the interview was very impressed with my books, had many insightful questions, and asked me to "stay on the line," which added fifteen more minutes to our segment, stretching a cost-free publicity opportunity from twenty to forty minutes. It was truly enjoyable and I felt very blessed by his generosity, but the best was yet to come. In the last two minutes of the broadcast, he announced that his employer would be hosting a holistic conference in the spring of the next year, and asked if I would accept his invitation to be a featured speaker there. I told him that I would be honored and delighted. After the idea had sunk in, I realized that this was what I had asked of the Universe: a sign that I should continue to pursue speaking opportunities. What better go sign than an opportunity to speak itself? As if that was not enough, the Spirit sealed the deal the next day, just in case I had any further doubts.

Professional speakers have top-notch videos of themselves presenting a speech that they use as their audition tape for prospective clients. Even though I was given this opportunity to speak without the use of a video, I still felt I might need to record one for future possible engagements. Again, it is costly, and I had no idea what went into it. I had been wondering how to get my hands on one, to use as an example in preparing for mine. The day after my radio interview, I received a CD-ROM in the mail. I was surprised by its arrival, because I had not sent for one. It came as they say, "out of the blue." Or did it? The CD-ROM turned out to be a directory of professional speakers available for hire and included their videos! I had not one example, but many, right in my hand! A second sign appeared telling me to keep going, and this little Italian-American gal never questions God!

Mind Signs

A chapter on soul searching would not be complete without some heavy duty scrutiny of our thoughts. Oftentimes, signs will not take the form of a tangible event, but rather, will be sent as inspired thought, or intuition. The sign may be something that you have deduced after experiencing a series of meaningful occurrences, such as poignant conversations, startling impressions you've received from your environment, or significantly unusual circumstances. I call these, "Mind Signs." All of us, at one time or another, have experienced them.

Again, my assistant, Ondrea, had a recent example of a mind sign. Recently, she was looking for a doctor in the yellow pages. After perusing the overwhelming advertisements, she saw an interesting and appropriate ad, and decided to make an appointment to see that doctor. During her appointment, the doctor asked her how she had heard of him, and she mentioned her telephone book search. As she tells it, he was taken aback for a moment. He said that he had seriously considered pulling that ad that very day. He went on to say that he thought this situation must be a sign advising him to keep the ad running. The fact that she had found such a spiritually aware physician was also a sign to Ondrea that she was in the right place! They both formed simple deductions based upon a rather interesting cosmic circumstance.

Over the years, I have found that mind signs tend to come to us most often through other people and the circumstances surrounding them. In the long run, it pays to listen to and observe our fellow man. You never know who will be your sign delivery person!

Mind signs are a bit more difficult to discern, but if you become adept at soul searching, you will not have any trouble at all figuring them out. All you really need to do is be aware. You might get tired of hearing this throughout this book, but awareness is a very important tool to recognizing and understanding all of your sacred signs, no matter what form they take.

Dream Signs

Dreams are the source of so much valuable information it is mind boggling. They are also the harbingers of sacred signs. Let us do a bit of soul searching in this area. Your dreams tell allegorical stories as they process information from your subconscious mind. Yet, they are a channel for spiritual information as well. The Universe uses our dreams to deliver its messages. Some of us are more receptive to this sort of medium than others, but I am certain that we all receive signs this way at some time or other.

You will most likely perceive your dream sign upon awakening, unless you are lucid dreaming. Lucid dreams are those in which we feel we are actually aware that we are dreaming. You have had one of these or more, for sure. They are the type of dreams in which you talk to yourself while asleep. You might say to yourself, "I know that this is a dream," or, "I'm dreaming now and I'll remember this when I get up," or, "Am I dreaming, because this feels real." Anyway, when you are having one of these lucid moments in dreamtime, signs are easy to discern. Do some soul searching of your own now, and try to remember when you have perceived a sign during or after a dream.

One of my dear students, Garth, had quite an enlightening experience with a dream sign. In fact, he got three all in the same night! To my knowledge and experience, that is a record! Garth was struggling with a career choice. He spent count-less hours worrying about what he should do to achieve his goal of finding a new career that would better reflect his personality, needs, and desires, and be more fulfilling.

It is an understatement to say that Garth is very handy around the house. He en-joys designing home rebuilding projects, and seeing them through to completion with his own hands. This work is joyful for him and quite fulfilling. He had an idea to pursue a new career buying property and renovating it for resale or rental pur-poses, but he wasn't sure which would be better and more harmonious for him. He turned to the Universe for his answer.

Garth asked for a sign requesting insight into what course he should pursue next concerning his new career. "I wanted to know what my next move should be," he told me, "and I wasn't quite sure which way to go." Then, one night, he had a dream. His dream showed him building an addition to a home. The intensity of the dream woke him up, leaving him with a nagging thought: what did that dream mean? Did it mean he should buy property, renovate, and then sell it, or should he buy, reno-vate, and rent? Being the good and faithful soul searcher he is, Garth wanted clarifi-cation. Right then and there, in the middle of the night, he asked for another very specific sign.

An adventurous soul, Garth asked to be shown one of two signs in his next clari-fying dream. If he was to buy, renovate and sell, he asked to see himself renovating a building. If he was to buy, renovate, and rent, he asked to see a building with several apartments in it for possible rentals. Then, he went right back to sleep. The same night, several hours later, he awoke with yet another sign! His dream showed him doing a renovation. Very clearly the sign indicated that he should buy, renovate, and sell, rather than rent.

Still unconvinced (Garth needs lots of proof, as do we all), he asked for yet an-other clarification sign! This guy was determined to get it right. His doubts were rea-sonable because the housing market in which we live is booming and it would take a lot of cash to get such a business going. He had a lot riding on this one, so I can't blame him for trying so hard.

FYI, everyone—it is okay to ask for more than one sign, as long as it pertains to the same subject. I will tell you more about that in Part II. But now, let's get back to the dreamtime adventures of Garth, the Renovator.

Back to sleep again, yet a third dream gave him the convincing he needed. In this one, he again saw himself renovating a building. Getting the same message more than once in three separate dreams, during the same sleep cycle finally did it for him. Even though it is a challenge in this market, Garth is pursuing his new career with absolute trust in Spirit and his dream signs.

Look back at your own dreams in your soul searching. Have you ignored your dream signs in the past? If so, make a promise to yourself to, yes, pay closer attention!

And, oh, sleep tight and pleasant dreams . . .

Here's Looking at You, Kid

During your soul searching, looking back at when and how your own signs have shown up in your life in the past is important to understanding how to utilize them in the future. One sunny afternoon, several years ago, I was driving down a country road thinking about calling an old friend whom I hadn't seen in years. Her name was Mary Ellen Roth, prior to her marriage. She and I were best friends for many years when I lived in Kansas. Yes, Dorothy, I lived in the beautiful state of Oz for nine years and came to love and treasure my every moment there. Anyway, I digress. Yes, the sign.

Mary Ellen and I had gotten in touch after I moved back to New York. She moved here as well, years later, so we were able to renew our friendship, but unfortunately we did not live close to each other. This day, I was driving alone thinking about her, and wondering if I should give her a call. About five or ten minutes later I passed a billboard that astounded me. On it was a picture of a young woman who happened to have been a local realtor. Next to her picture were the words, "Call Mary Ellen Roth today for a great deal on your home!" Okay, so what do you think of that? Luck? Coincidence? Guess what I did when I got home?

Have situations like that happened to you when you least expected them? It is time to think back now with an exercise that will help you draw these signs back to your consciousness. In doing so, you'll prepare yourself for more intense sign work. This exercise should sharpen your powers of awareness.

Soul Searching Exercises

This exercise is designed to help you look back and recognize the times when sacred signs have made themselves known in your life. Answer the questions objectively, and take your time with them. You might need to begin this exercise and come back to it later, if you run into a mental block. Just relax and breathe, and the information will come to you. Once again, you may record your answers to these exercises here or on the blank pages in the section at the back of this book called, "Sacred Sign Journal."

Exercise #3

1. Allow your mind to think back to a time in your recent past, one or two years ago, when you were surprised by an event that occurred that seemed like a coincidence to you. To help you call it to mind, think about a happy, surprising event, or one that had a great impact on your life at the time. Record it.

when Dr. Toohey told me my TT. would be life changing.

2. What were the circumstances surrounding that event? How did the event unfold? When you think about it, can you see a pattern in the way the events leading to the final result occurred? Describe it.

I had been visualizing a flat tummy & pulling up my skin for years.

3. Now think of another unusual and surprising incident that happened earlier in your life, say five years ago. Record and describe it as you did in numbers 1 and 2.

got a bug up my butt, quit sc & went to Sicily one of the best decisions I've made

4. Open your consciousness to yet another event, but this time allow your mind to go as far back in time as it chooses. Record and describe this event as above.

when I finally decided to move out of OK because of Donny Lotts

5. Now think back to a very moving and transformational dream you might have had in the past. How were you impacted by this dream? Did it move you to action in any way, or seem to solve a problem you were thinking about? Did it feel "real"? Record your impressions.

Dreamt I drove to Jens house in fullerton & it was completely dark.

Your answers may have taken a bit of time to discern. It is fine to take as much time as you need because you are not merely looking back at an event, you're analyzing a process. That takes time. Let us do a bit more soul searching and study your answers.

- Was it easier for you to think back one or two years, or was it simpler to go way back?

- Were the memories happy or sad, surprising or not?

- Were you aware of what was happening at the time the events were revealing themselves?

- Did you have an indication of what was going to happen before it did? (Sometimes signs will be revealed to announce that a sign is about to be revealed!)

- Were the events you recalled preceded by any strong thought that you might have had? What were you thinking days, hours, minutes, before the event occurred?

- Did you realize at the time that a dream was trying to tell you something?

If the events from your recent past, one or two years ago, were easier for you to discern, this is an indication that you are probably very aware and conscious of what is happening around you. If it is easier for you to recall events further into the past, then you probably have a good long-term memory and have been aware of strange and usual happenings in your life for some time. There is no right or wrong response here. You are doing this exercise to acquaint you with your own powers of observation and memory.

As in the above analysis, if you tend to remember more happy events than sad ones, you might be blocking some important information from coming to you. Remember that our learning occurs not only from joyful circumstances but from negative ones as well. It is important to be aware of all events, good or bad, so that you may use the lessons you learn for spiritual growth, and to recognize warning signs when they may arrive.

A sign might precede a sign. For instance, days before I saw the billboard with my friend's name on it and received my sign to call her, I was watching a television show with a segment on how a woman rented a huge billboard and used it as a personal ad to find a mate. Apparently, she got a lot of press and thousands of responses from men who had driven by it. If my attention had not been turned to billboards by that show, a clear sign that a sign was on the way, I might not have even noticed the one with my friend's name on it. Generally I ignore most billboards, but that day, after having seen the show, I paid more attention to them than usual. Good thing! So, has a sign preceded your sign or event?

Finally, when you're soul searching and trying to examine your awareness of spiritual signs in your world, you need to put some emphasis upon what you were thinking. I have been adamant about stressing to my students and clients that thought produces tangible results, so I will not waver here. What you are thinking is crucial to what occurs in the flesh. To help with recognizing sacred signs, when you are soul searching, put time into examining your thoughts prior to the surprising, synchronistic events that enter your life.

The analysis of your recall will help you to become knowledgeable about how signs might have already appeared to you, and as you write your responses and later read them, you will probably think of others. Once those floodgates are opened, get ready for the big waves! In your soul-searching efforts, chat with your friends about signs they might have received and compare notes. Other people are always willing to tell you about such things, because they find them exciting and unusual. I am hoping by the time you finish your spiritual search, you will find the occurrence of sacred signs common in your life in the past, and a continuing part of your everyday existence.

More Soul Searching

Nope, your job is not over yet. There is more work to be done to help you understand your receptivity to sacred messages. Here is an exercise to help.

Exercise #4

It is time to get down to specifics. In this exercise you are asked to write down any and all sacred signs you might think have ever come to you. The catch is not to hold back anything. Even if you are not sure that something was really a sign, record it anyway. Do not censor anything. This might take quite some time, but I assure you the effort is worth the trouble. You might be missing your messages because you simply do not know what to look for, so turn a clean page in the journal and write away!

1. To the best of your ability, write down any and all signs, synchronistic events, or unusual occurrences that have been a part of your life.

Donnie letts blowing me off me applyjng for a job at Typon food & realizing I had to heave OK

2. For each one, note the following (if you have trouble remembering the specifics, don't worry, just come up with an approximate answer):
   a. the year it happened,   *1984*
   b. how old you were,   *25*

c. what was going on in your life at the time,

d. and how you felt about the sign at the moment it occurred.

was sick of living w/mom
& wanted my independence
Donnie kicked me off,
not being able to get a decent job

3. Record the action you took as a result of receiving your message/sign.

left OK, moved to FL 1 month
& then moved to Brooklyn

4. How was your life changed?

met Jim, became a widow,
moved to CA, quit smoking
book job a TV

   Looking back at your answers, you should be able to see a distinct result of the sign. I was moved by the billboard with my friend's name on it, and the fact that I acted upon it and called her brought joy to both of us. That consequently strengthened our friendship, and further led me to never discount my spiritual messages. Do the same sort of examination of each of your signs. What impact have they had on you and on your spiritual awareness and growth? How old were you when you began to realize that such signs existed? Most importantly, be honest with yourself. Are you are a believer or do you still need more convincing?

   If your impressions are still not coming easily from your subconscious, I have a meditation for you. You may do it to open your mind to more insightful information from your past that will help in your future sacred message work. I have found that, besides relaxation, these simple meditations clear away the clutter in our minds and draw insights to our consciousness that we might not have otherwise discerned. Try this one.

Soul Searching Meditation

Find a comfortable position in your chair, hands on your lap, and feet flat on the floor. Close your eyes and take three gentle breaths, inhaling through the nose, and exhaling through the mouth. . . . Continue breathing gently with mouth closed. As you do, feel a wave of relaxation moving from the top of your head, slowly down, down, down, to the tip of your toes. . . . Breathe gently and focus your mind on a pleasant memory from your past. Do not try to force a memory or attempt to conjure one, but rather, allow your mind to drift peacefully to a time in your past that was loving and joyful for you. . . . Accept the thoughts that surround this image by opening to the circumstances that led to this event. Silently ask yourself, "How did this event come to be?. . . . What were the moments of significance that led up to this happy time?. . . . Do I see a pattern unfolding?. . . . Were there signs that I did not recognize then, that I can see now?". . . . Just reflect on those questions for a bit, and let the answers be revealed to you from you higher consciousness. . . . When you feel your answers have been made clear to you, and you are ready and at peace, take a gentle breath, and as you exhale, open your eyes.

If you wish, record the information you received in this meditation in the sacred sign journal.

Soul Searching Affirmation

Thank you, God/Goddess/Spirit/Universe, for opening my mind and heart to what has shaped my life in the past. I take an objective look back at my choices, and accept my responsibility in the creation of my life as it is now. What went before is freely available to me in my divine mind, comes to me easily, and I use the information for my highest good. And so it is!

Important Points to Remember

- You need to take some time to analyze your own past history concerning signs.

- It takes confidence to do sign work.

- Synchronicity is active in our lives, and the events therein are not random.

- We have a measure of control over the appearance of synchronicities in our world.

- Synchronicity is the method the Universe uses to channel your sacred signs to you.

- You must pay attention!

- Luck is a result of efforts put forth by intention and will.

- Sacred signs do not depend upon luck. They depend upon directed effort, spiritual fortitude, and trust.

- Negative signs you do not want sometimes appear.

- Stop signs are clear indicators that we should consider not doing what we have planned to do.

- Go signs help us make decisions, indicate that we should proceed with an action, or notify us that we are on the right track in our efforts.

- Go signs answer "yes/no" questions.

- Mind signs are sent as inspired thought or intuition, or are deduced through a series of meaningful occurrences.

- Dream signs are those which we receive in our dreamtime hours, and are literal or allegorical in nature.

- Look back at how and when your own signs have shown up in your life by doing your personal soul searching.

- A sign might precede a sign.

- What you were thinking prior to receiving a sign is crucial to its manifestation.

Chapter Three

Three Mistake-Proof Keys to the Knowledge of the Universe

As I have promised, I have tested and proven several surefire, mistake-proof ways to discern and make sense of your sacred signs. These steps are very easy to master. I call them the "Keys to the Knowledge of the Universe," and I am more than happy to share them with you now. Remember to keep an open mind, and remind yourself that you are strong enough and skilled enough just as you are, to master them. The keys are as follows:

- Ask
- Accept
- Trust

Yes, my friends. That is it. These three little words might appear to be innocent as you gaze at them, but they are quite powerful in practice. When you attempt to put these steps into action, it will be a true test of spiritual fortitude, because just as with any other important undertaking, you will need to commit to your work. Asking, accepting, and trusting seem to be uncomplicated tasks, but when you relate them to the Universe, they require a great deal of courage to enact. I know you have what it takes, and I sure hope you do! Once you dedicate your efforts to recognizing and understanding the ways in which the Universe communicates, you unleash a plethora of good in your life. Tuning into your sacred signs can enable you to increase your joy on every level of your existence. You will begin a communication with a Divine force that wants you to have your heart's desires and will help you attain them. Mastering these remarkable tools will be worth all the effort you put into it.

I will give you the details of using the three keys in Part II of this book, but for now, let's try to understand what's in store by way of an overview of each of them.

Key #1: Ask

Asking is the first key to working with sacred signs. For many of us, it is hard to ask for anything, especially something from God/Universe. We have a historically based fear of the wrath of the Lord descending upon us if we screw up, so it is understandable that we might be reluctant to make our wants known. Yet, if we can but muster the courage, we will be astounded at the results.

Requesting knowledge from the Universe is a scary task for several reasons. We might not feel deserving. There is the "Why Would God Talk to Me" syndrome, which is quite common among us. Then there is the "This Is a Lot of Baloney" syndrome, also prevalent. And then there is the "What Do I Do if I Really Do Get a Sign" syndrome, which is my particular favorite.

Well, addressing these fears individually, first, I would say that God/Goddess/ Spirit/Universe is not all that particular about to whom he/she speaks. Author Neale Donald Walsh, of the *Conversations with God* books, does not have a hotline to heaven, and he would be the first to say that. God will talk to any one of us, because Spirit loves us equally and we are equally blessed. We all have the gift within each of us to communicate with the Divine. We were born with it. How we choose to use that gift is up to us. My suggestion is we use it to live a better life by opening to the messages that the Creator is trying to send us. We humans are thickheaded and really need a jolt to get us going sometimes. That is why the sacred signs sometimes appear so startling to us. We are just not ready for them. However, when we are ready, even though the signs might still be startling, we will know what they mean and how to use them, if we choose to learn to do so.

Second, I understand that these concepts may be fair game to debunkers. (Is the Amazing Randy within earshot?) There will always be folks who do not believe. That is what makes life interesting. Yet even people who think that taking the time to develop a skill to uncover messages from the Universe is crazy will also receive them. That is the beauty of unconditional love. Our Creator supplies us all, believers or nonbelievers alike. Now, I'm taking for granted that you are a believer because you are reading this far into the book, so I will take the liberty of saying that even if you, a believer, have trouble believing in your own signs, by the end of this book your doubts and fears will be resolved. Isn't that something to look forward to?

Third, there is the matter of what to do if you ask for a sign and actually do receive one. This is probably the most daunting of the three syndromes. Asking is one thing, and receiving is another. Even the Bible tells us that if we ask we will surely receive. It does not tell us what decisions to make or how to proceed because God does not interfere with our free will. So, what do we do if we get a sign? Believe it for one thing, and do not be afraid that you will not know what to do. If the Universe sends you a sign, it always sends you the means to act upon it. You get to choose to act or not. You are guided to your highest good if you pay attention, and follow the prompting of the sign in an open and loving manner. With right intention, you cannot go wrong. Do not worry that you will not know what to do if you get a sign when you ask for one. Simply ask and watch as the Universe leads you to a positive result.

Questions About Asking

When you ask for a sign to appear in your world or your consciousness, you are opening a channel to higher realms. That bears great responsibility, so do not ask if you do not plan to follow through. We should always strive to send the best possible messages back into the Universe, so not heeding the signs we receive sends the message that we do not trust them, which, in turn, causes the Universe to send more reasons not to trust them, and that would be a pity. That is why many people say, "I ask for plenty of signs, but I never get them. What's up with that?" Well, they might have repeatedly ignored the signs, misused them, or distrusted them, so they receive more reasons to ignore, misuse, or distrust. You get back what you send. So find the courage to ask for your signs, and be ready to put their messages into action in your life.

In doing sign work, there are inevitably many questions in our minds. Here are some of the most common I have heard in the almost two decades I have been doing this work:

- Why is it important to ask for signs?

- What should I ask for?

- When should I ask?

- Who should ask for signs?

- Where or in what physical environment should I ask for a sign?

By way of clarification, I will take each one of these questions and hopefully alleviate some of your doubts and fears in the process.

Why is it important to ask for signs?

It is very important to ask for sacred signs to be manifest into our lives because they are vital tools in living a life of joy, abundance, love, and prosperity. The Universe has all the answers, in case you did not already know that. Go straight to the Source of *everything* for the answers to your most pressing or even mundane questions. I do. God/Goddess does not want to interfere in our lives without our permission (that free will thing again), and will not impose his or her will on any of us. But if we *request* Spirit's intervention, we will most assuredly get it. Look at it in the following way.

A parent sometimes feels she or he knows what is best for their child, but she does not intervene in that child's life so that he or she may learn their lessons in his own way. Think about that loser boyfriend you had in high school that made your parents' blood boil, but they were powerless to stop you from dating him, so they stood back, watched, and let you learn your own lesson when he dumped you. God works that way, too. The Universe stands by and allows us to make our own decisions and choices, until, or unless, we ask for help. As we grow in spiritual understanding, we learn to ask for help before it is too late rather than after the fact, just as we did as teens when we nursed that broken heart and blamed our parents' lack of intervention for it—"Why didn't you tell me he was a bum and stop me from dating him?" Do you see the picture? Asking for your sacred signs is so important because they can help you avoid pain and struggle. If you ask for them early on when you are contemplating a situation, you get a much more fulfilling and better result.

What should I ask for?

Ask for anything. This is an easy question to answer. The Universe wants you to have the things you desire and to live the life of your dreams. Therefore, nothing is beyond the scope of a request. I remember several years ago when I was working as a weather anchor at a local cable station in my hometown, one of my associates asked me what he thought to be a loaded question, but I safely dodged the bullet with my answer, and I know he didn't like it.

In a conversation we were having before we went on air, we were discussing God, as we frequently did. I am an interfaith, metaphysical minister, and he was a devout Christian, so our conversations were interesting, albeit spirited. He wanted to know why I believed that God wants us to have everything we desire. He felt that, as a parent himself, he did not want his children to think that they could get anything they want in life, because he felt that would be giving them false hope, or indulging them in some way. He felt he would be spoiling them and they would grow up to be selfish, inconsiderate people. To his way of thinking, God agrees with him, and we therefore have to suffer, struggle, be in lack or in pain to become "better people." He believed that if we could and did acquire everything we ever wanted we would not need God, and that was that.

My answer was that God created us in his image and placed us upon the Earth to live a joyful, abundant, prosperous life. We are the ones who screwed that up by making seriously unwise choices. I told him I believed that in God's eyes we were already perfect, wonderful children, and did not need to become "better people." We only need to become better when we have been at our worst, and that, too, is our choice. I am not sure I got through to him, but you can see my point. The Universe gives us the opportunity to choose the life we desire—one of abundance and joy, or one of pain and struggle. God does not dictate the road for us to take, we get to pick it, and in so doing we create our future. God stands back and lets us do life the way we see fit, always ready to lead us back to the Light. Spirit offers us the best, and it is our choice to either take it or leave it. We design our lives through the actions, thoughts, and decisions we make each day. Everything is available to us for the asking, so construct your request for a sacred sign wisely.

When should I ask?

This is another easy one. You should ask when you are in need. For some of us that is quite often, and for others not. Ask for a sacred sign whenever you have a dilemma or problem to solve, need to make an important decision, or just need general guidance on a subject. The more you ask *with sincere intention*, the more you will receive. Do not ask just because you think it is "cool," or because you are a spiritual junkie and cannot get enough psychic information, because those are not sincere intentions; they are indulgences, and you will not get the results you desire.

Who should ask for signs?

Anyone may ask for signs. You do not have to believe in psychic manifestations, or be an avid spiritual seeker. All those with a heartfelt desire to receive divine guidance are perfect candidates for sign work. It does help immeasurably if you have some metaphysical knowledge already, because it enhances your work, but it is not necessary. The novice and advanced student are equally as capable, given the proper tools to make the job easier.

Where or in what physical environment should I ask for a sign?

I truly believe that one should be alone, in a private, serene environment when asking for sacred signs. I feel it is necessary to have as few distractions as possible around you, so you may focus all of your energy and form a powerful intention. It is difficult to do that in a crowd, so try to be alone, or do the asking when your household is asleep and you have some private, quiet time. In chapter 4, I will talk about some private rituals you might want to create when doing your sign work, but all it really takes is a peaceful, quiet mind.

Key #2: Accept

Acceptance is a difficult thing to do for many of us. Even though we might want to believe with all our heart that if we ask for a small miracle we will receive it, it is still hard for us to accept that such a thing is possible. I guess we have to look back at our upbringing to see just how skeptical we are. It makes sense that if you had a challenging life as a child you would be less apt to accept that which you cannot see. Those of us raised in traditional religions would find it easier to accept the appearance of signs because they are part of religious Judeo-Christian teachings. If we were not raised in such an environment, it will take a bit more time to not only accept that receiving signs from the Universe is possible, but also to recognize them once they appear. It might help all of us to see this idea explained through a few careful questions.

- How do sacred signs appear in my physical world?
- Do I have the power, intellect, or spiritual knowledge to recognize signs?
- When a sign appears, will I know it?
- How will I know it is truly a sign and not just my vivid imagination?

Let us take a look at those questions to clarify this second important key to the Universe.

How do sacred signs appear in my physical world?

The first thing to understand is that signs are as individual as the people who ask for them. Signs will appear in your physical world through a series of energy responses that work together to materialize your request into physical form. You may literally move matter or substance with your mind. Have you ever used a pendulum? You might try it and you will understand what I mean. Let me tell you a story.

Recently, I was teaching a class in which I was lecturing on the power of the energy of the mind. My students were as doubtful as I am sure some of you are at this moment, but when they saw the physical demonstration, they were awestruck. The point was simple but astounding.

I began by holding a wooden pendulum suspended from a string in my right hand. I held my right arm steady with my left hand to keep it from directing the movement of the pendulum. As the pendulum dangled from my fingers, I willed it to move. My intention was to have it turn in a circular clockwise direction. As I concentrated, and as my incredulous students watched, the pendulum slowly began to move. At first, it moved in a small circle, but within seconds, it began to make sweeping circles so large that the pendulum actually hit my arm as it swung. I wish I'd had a camera that day, because you should have seen the expressions on the faces of those students. They could not believe it. With eyes as big as saucers, they relented and agreed what I posited was possible. To drive the point home even further, I told them that I also had the mental power to make the pendulum stop at will. "This we've gotta see," they mused. So, as I focused my attention, the pendulum slowly came to a dead stop, once again dangling peacefully and motionless from my hand.

It did not take long for the students to realize that if my mind could conduct energy down my body to an inanimate object and make it move, it is possible to extend that energy, and move matter elsewhere in the Universe. That is essentially what is happening when you ask for a sacred sign. You send energy into the cosmos that is so precise that the dominant vibration alters the vibration of the object you focus upon. You have heard of spoon bending, I presume. Alternately, if you ask, as I do, for a penny to appear when you need reassurance that all is well, that intention is so focused it literally transports a penny into your circle of influence or energy path. I am not quoting scientific data here, but rather spiritual belief, based upon centuries of psychic observation.

That is how signs appear in your physical world. Of course, the other explanation is that the appearance of sacred signs is nothing short of a miracle. You decide.

*Do I have the power, intellect, or spiritual knowledge to recognize
signs?*

Yes. You are alive and breathing, are you not? Spiritually we are all equal in the
eyes of God. The power to recognize signs requires a willing heart. You do not need
to be a genius or avid spiritual seeker to become aware of them. What is also required on your part is a commitment to awareness, to paying attention to what is
happening in the world around you. If you are sensitive to changes in your immediate environment, really listen to what people are saying around you, and identify as
meaningful occurrences the unusual circumstances that you would otherwise cate-
gorize as coincidence, you will be exercising this innate power, and using it to its
fullest to decipher your spiritual messages.

When a sign appears, will I know it?

This answer is a simple one. Of course, you will know it is a sign because you have
asked for it specifically. If you ask for a particular flower to appear as a sign, as did
my client, you will see that particular flower, either in the flesh or in a written word;
hear it through music or in someone's loving advice; or experience it in any number
of practical demonstrations.

One of the most startling things about working with signs is that they are immediately recognizable to the one who asked for them. Even if you are not quite sure,
do not talk yourself out of that pleasure by rationalizing. Rather, think about the
odds of that specific sign appearing in a designated amount of time. We will talk
more about timing later on, but it is enough to say that such machinations are not
merely coincidental. In time, and after seeing positive results repeatedly, you will
come to accept them.

How will I know it is truly a sign and not just my vivid imagination?

Of all these questions, this is perhaps the one most asked. To accept that you received a sacred sign takes faith. Once you have undertaken to pursue this method of
communication with the Universe, you must take certain concepts on faith, understanding with quiet assurance that you are indeed conversing with God. A spiritual
seeker does this with ease, so if you find yourself in this category, you should have no

trouble believing that a sign has appeared when it has made itself obvious to you. If you still have doubt, then you must continue asking for signs and for obvious clarity, so you will see and then believe. The Universe is willing to work with you on that one.

One of the pitfalls of the skeptic is the constant attempt to justify with logic all occurrences, natural or otherwise. Some things are just not quantifiable. Sacred signs are some of them. Therefore, it would not be worth all the mental energy you would need to expend to determine the validity of a sign. My advice is to accept as real what you see with your own eyes, and what you perceive with your senses. Do not try to justify your doubt by telling yourself that your imagination is to blame.

Key #3: Trust

The third and final key is trust. Trusting in sacred signs is more than just believing that they are possible. Rather, it is knowing beyond the shadow of a doubt that you are loved and protected by a force in the Universe that is always there to hear and answer your requests, no matter how simple or complex they may be. Trust asks us to abandon our naturally conditioned way of thinking. It asks us to make the transition from logic to a more abstract or global way of perceiving life. *In essence, when we truly trust we stop trying to figure things out.* We end the habit of fretting over problems and instinctively know that solutions are not far away. You can see why trust comes after acceptance in the keys. Once you have accepted that sacred messages from the Universe do appear in your life, you need to trust that they are true and valid, and take action based upon them. Until you trust that the signs you are receiving are actually happening, you will be hesitant to make changes in your life.

Here are some commonly asked questions regarding trust:

- How do I begin to trust in the Universe, when it does not seem real and tangible to me?

- Is there a way to stop my doubting thoughts that seem to recur?

- Why am I afraid to trust in the sacred signs?

- What happens if I follow a sign and things do not work out happily?

Trust is the primary focus of chapter six, but for now the answers to these questions should prove helpful.

How do I begin to trust in the Universe, when it does not seem real and tangible to me?

I realize that it is tough to believe in something you cannot see, touch, feel, taste, or smell. In short, it just does not seem real. Therefore, if the Universe is not real to you, you will have difficulty respecting the advice it gives. You must begin to see the Universe, your Creator, as a tangible energy. Look around you. The Earth is abundant with God's creations. Spend time thinking about the wonders of nature. Even your arrival on the planet was an astounding happening in itself. Consider how miraculous your personal talents and those of others are. Music is tangible evidence of the existence of God, as is art, literature, poetry, and the laughter of children. There is so much substantial evidence that God/Goddess exists, if you just take the time to recognize it.

Is there a way to stop my doubting thoughts that seem to recur?

We humans will always have doubt. Doubt is necessary to our spiritual growth because it teaches us about faith. Do not reprimand yourself for having doubts. Instead, accept that questioning is part of your nature, and make a choice not to allow it to dominate your thoughts. People tend to define their world by what they think are facts. For instance, if you eat a lot of food you will get fat. That is what most of us believe, yet there are very many people who are thin and eat a lot. Individual metabolism and other specific factors come into play. The issue is neither black nor white, but gray. Therefore, doubt, at its best, keeps us from making judgments.

You can squelch those nagging negative thoughts by replacing them with other, more constructive ones. Whenever you have a thought that expresses doubt, you stop your good from coming to you. You must take action to keep your channels of spirit communication open. Here is what you may do to keep that positive energy flowing:

- Stop expecting that you will not get the sign you have requested. Expect success.

All prayers are answered. The only way you will not get the sacred sign is if you are not using the tools you learn here, and are unaware of it.

- Do a bit of self-talk and affirm, "I am always aware of my sacred signs when they manifest in my life."

This builds confidence and fights doubt. You should repeat this whenever you feel those questionable moments coming on and until you believe it!

- Do not tell others about your sign until it manifests.

Other people tend to discourage us with their own doubt. There is nothing like hearing, "That sign stuff is a lot of hooey!" to throw a wrench into your thinking.

If you are faithful and follow these tips when you ask for your signs, you will experience your doubt subsiding and enjoy a feeling of peace and healthy anticipation.

Why am I afraid to trust in the sacred signs?

Along with doubt, fear will put an end to your perceiving your sacred signs. When we are fearful, we lack trust, the most important key to appreciating our communications from the Universe. It takes time to build trust when there is no climate of fear present, so when fear does exist it is even harder. There are many reasons why we are afraid to trust in signs. In my years of doing this work, I have come to recognize certain common fears among the people I counsel. Most people are afraid to trust their messages for the following reasons:

- We are afraid that we will be judged as silly, crazy, weird, or blasphemous.

- We are afraid of losing control to an unseen force. (Who really is it that is sending us the sign?)

- We are afraid that the guidance of a sign is faulty.

- We are afraid that we will misinterpret or not understand the guidance.

- We are afraid the guidance is leading us to do something against our will.

- We are afraid we are conjuring up negative spirits or events.

These are six of the most-often expressed fears. I know there are more, but let us address each of them. Facing the fears is the best way to put an end to them.

- We are afraid that we will be judged as silly, crazy, weird, or blasphemous.

It is a valid fear that others will think ill of us in some fashion if we put our trust into an unseen energy or a belief that is not common or popular. Yes, there will always be folks who think you are misled or dealing in nonsense, or even sinning, depending upon your cultural and religious upbringing. You must decide for yourself how you will handle the comments of others should you continue to work with signs. As I have previously mentioned, it might be wise not to say anything to anyone, not only before your sign appears, but also after. Unless you are blessed to be in an environment where others think the way you do, you might just be setting yourself up for criticism. Only you can make that determination. Signs are harmless. They will never hurt you or anyone else. What you do with the guidance they give creates harmony or chaos, and I hope you are good at the former and have given up the latter! It is all in your hands.

- We are afraid of losing control to an unseen force. (Who really is it that is sending us the sign?)

There is no bogey man delivering the messages. No demon or negative spirit is involved with a sacred sign. That would hardly be sacred, would it? God/Spirit/Goddess/Universe/All There Is, etc. which is *within you*, is the source of the information and YOU are also the magnet that attracts that information, so do not put any further energy into fretting about where the signs come from. *Nothing and no one, on this plane or the next, is or ever will be able to overpower your mind and spirit unless you allow it.*

- We are afraid that the guidance of a sign is faulty.

This is another easy fear to address. The guidance that comes from and to us from our higher consciousness comes from that which we recognize as God, whom we also recognize as infallible. It can never be wrong!

- We are afraid that we will misinterpret or not understand the guidance.

This fear relates to our self-confidence and self-worth. You need to have the confidence in your ability to learn the techniques to interpret your signs, and the energy and focus to act upon them. If you allow your intuition to help you understand the message when it comes into your reality, instead of allowing your head to debunk it, you will have no problem interpreting a sacred sign.

- We are afraid the guidance is leading us to do something against our will.

Again, you are in full control of your spiritual self at all times. There is nothing outside of you that can overpower your free will in any way. Besides, a sacred sign will never send a message to you to hurt yourself or someone else. If you ask for such signs, you need to see a psychiatrist right away!

- We are afraid we are conjuring up negative spirits or events.

When you ask for a sacred sign you are asking God to send guidance. It is not the same as playing with a Ouija Board, or invoking the spirits of the dead to do your bidding. No negative entity will invade. Of course, we know there are negative energies in the Universe, but you are not even close to conjuring them by asking for confirmation through a sign, as long as your intentions are pure. By the same token, you will not set yourself up for negative events to occur in your life, nor will you be inflicting the same on anyone else.

Let us get back to this issue of trust. Release fear, and trust is a natural result.

What happens if I follow a sign and things do not work out happily?

Sometimes acting on the guidance we receive may seem to cause the situation to turn out badly. We do not know the entire picture of our lives as God does. It is our destiny on Earth to be students and to learn our lessons well. Sometimes we will receive a sign to proceed with a situation we thought would bring us joy, but it eventually ends painfully. For example, this point is demonstrated if we receive guidance to marry, and then divorce occurs in the future. Such a happening does not mean you were led astray by your higher self. It simply means your spirit needed to receive that guidance in order for you to be in the position to learn the lesson that your soul wished to learn. If the sign had not guided you to your action, it would have influenced your free will, which is not the message God would ever send!

Mistake-Proof Exercise

It is time for you to examine your commitment to working with sacred signs. The following exercise will help you move past any blocks you might have to receiving your signs, and to trust in the help from the Universe. If you are totally honest with yourself in answering these questions, you will see a pattern of behavior emerging. You cannot make a mistake in answering these questions, so you should feel comfortable responding objectively. Again, as before, relax, breathe, and allow the answers to come naturally to you without undue stress or strain. Record them here or in the journal at the back of this book.

Exercise #5

1. Do you find it easy to ask for help when you need it from family and friends? If not, why do think that it is so? How does the act of asking for help make you feel?

No, I'm reluctant to impose on people, only ask help from dear friends, asking for help (if I really need it) makes me feel powerless

2. Are you a "control freak" and have a strong need to manage all circumstances of your life? Why do you think this is so?

Yes very much so, if I manage all aspects of my life I don't get hurt

3. Are you fearful of what others might think of you if you choose to work directly with the Universe? Do you feel you will be ridiculed? Why and by whom? (Be honest with this one!)

No, this part I don't care what others think

4. Are you brave enough to allow your higher spiritual power to take precedence over your logical mind? For example, have you ever relied on your "gut" feeling to make a decision? If you have ever done so, describe the incident now.

my gut is never wrong
my gut told me to do this
17, move to NY, dump jim,
& that Janitor Jim was lying to me

Analyze Your Answers

Question #1 is guiding you to understand your willingness to work with signs and to feel comfortable doing so. If you are someone who has trouble asking for help, then you might not be at ease working with signs. Feelings of distrust, inadequacy, obligation, etc., hold many people back from asking for help. This is a block that needs to be removed. God wants to help us and to see us succeed, and awaits our requests. Does "ask and you shall receive" ring a bell?

Question #2 examines your ability to trust. If you do not have a strong desire to directly control all the aspects of your life, than you will do well working with signs. If you do have control issues, as they are called, you will be blocking your consciousness from accepting the signs when they appear. In which case, you must say the affirmation at the end of this chapter to help remove the block.When you find that you no longer feel the need to control life with such intensity, you will be ready to proceed.

Accepting that your signs are true indicators of messages from Spirit and trusting them requires that you release any thoughts of fear from your mind. Question #3 helps you to look at how you truly feel about what others think. If you are worried that you will be teased or discounted by family and friends, it will be very hard to work with signs because their doubts will inevitably work their way into your consciousness and you could miss some very helpful information along the way. Remember that others need not know about your sign work. It is up to you to share that information or not. I'm sure God will stay quiet on the subject!

Question #4 poses the greatest challenge to trusting in your sacred signs. Abandoning logic is one of the most difficult things we Western thinkers must do as we work in communication with the Divine. Start small, but begin to let your "gut" tell you what to do. I guarantee that you will be pleasantly surprised at how accurate it is.

Mistake-Proof Meditation

Find a comfortable position in your chair, hands on your lap, and feet flat on the floor. Close your eyes and take three gentle breaths, inhaling through the nose, and exhaling through the mouth. . . . Continue breathing gently with mouth closed. As you do, feel a wave of relaxation moving from the top of your head, slowly down, down, down, to the tip of your toes. . . . Breathe gently and tell yourself that you are safe and divinely protected. . . . Know that all you do is guided by a loving energy that will assist you in all your needs and lead you to your ultimate joy. . . . Release feelings of suspicion or doubt in your ability to communicate with the Universe, and tell yourself you will welcome all messages that come to you in a kind and loving way. . . . As you continue to breathe gently, inhale peace and tranquility and exhale all doubt and fear. You are a child of the Universe and it is here to help you now. Welcome it. . . . Relax in this moment of peace for a bit. . . . When you are ready, take another gentle breath, and as you exhale, return to consciousness and open your eyes.

If you wish, you may record your response to this meditation in the sacred sign journal at the back of this book.

Mistake-Proof Affirmation

*I now release any and all feelings of doubt or fear and readily accept my divine right to directly communicate with You, God/Goddess/Spirit/Universe. The sacred signs that I **ask** for and attract in my highest and greatest good come into my life without blocks or obstacles of any kind. I am profoundly grateful, **accept** all of them with courage, and I **trust** that they are true and perfect for me. And so it is!*

Important Points to Remember

- The three Mistake-Proof Keys to the Knowledge of the Universe are:

    Ask

    Accept

    Trust

- In order to work with the Keys effectively we must agree to eliminate fear.

- When you ask for a sign, you must be prepared to follow through with action.

- It is important to ask for signs because they are vital tools in living a life of joy, abundance, love, and prosperity.

- You may ask for anything.

- Ask for a sign when you are in need of guidance, have a dilemma or problem to solve, or need to make an important decision.

- You must ask with a sincere intention.

- Anyone may ask for signs.

- Ask for signs when you are alone, in a private, serene environment.

- Accept that it is truly possible for sacred signs to appear in your world.

- Signs appear through a series of energy responses.

- Believe that you have the power, intellect, and spiritual knowledge to recognize signs.

- You will always know when a sign has appeared.

- Try not to justify the appearance of a sign with logical thought as though it were simply a result of your imagination. It is not.

- Trust means knowing beyond the shadow of a doubt that you are loved.

- See the Universe, your Creator, as a tangible, living energy.

- Accept that doubts will surface, and choose not to allow them to dominate your thoughts.

- Expect success in your sacred sign work.

- Affirm: "I am always aware of my signs when they manifest in my life."

- Do not tell others about your sign until it manifests.

- It takes time to appreciate and trust in your signs. Eventually, you will.

- Do not allow your fears to control your spirit.

- When requested with sincere intention, the guidance given by your sacred sign is always in your highest good.

Using the Keys to Face and Challenge the Universe

Chapter Four

Key #1—Ask:
How to Request a Sacred Sign

You cannot get an answer if you do not ask a question, so now it is time to begin actively working with signs. With this first key, you will learn to open the door to your communication with Spirit. It is an exciting adventure and one I know you are now ready to pursue. In asking for your sign, you must know what to ask for, how to ask for it, and how to get that message to the Universe most effectively. In this chapter, you will discover all the information you will need to put your intentions and desires into words that have a direct impact upon your physical world.

Knowledge Is Power

It is very important to know what you want. For example, you may ask for a sign guiding you either to take an action or not. "Is it in my best interest to buy a new car, at this time, or should I wait?" might be the dilemma that is the priority in your life right now. "Should I buy a new or used car?" might also come to mind. In order to receive accurate guidance, you must decide which of these questions applies to your desired outcome, or what it is you truly want. That will help to form your intention. If you focus on the first question, the implication is that you are not sure the timing is right for you to purchase a car, and you want the Universe to tell you what to do. The second question implies that you have already decided to buy a car, but are not sure which type to purchase. The difference in these questions is significant because you would be essentially making two different requests. You must be clear on what you want before you ask for a sign to guide you in the decision-making process.

There is a process you must consistently follow when working with signs. You must always know what you want, and then form the request carefully to achieve an answer that will guide you accurately. Let us look at another example.

You might be wrestling with a choice to make concerning your career. Your thoughts might be, "Should I stay in my current career or make a total change?" or, "Should I take the job at _____, or the one at _____?" These are two totally different requests. If you wish to go into a new line of work, your intention is to change careers completely. On the other hand, if you have a choice between two jobs in your current line of work, then your intention is to receive guidance to help you make a specific choice. So you see, it is vital to know what type of guidance you want when asking for a sign.

Intention

The concept of intention is extremely important when doing sign work. When we do any work with Spirit/Universe we must do so with the idea that we honestly want the guidance, trust in it, and will follow it. Most importantly, we must intend that whatever we ask for results in the highest good for all those concerned, as well as ourselves. That is what makes these requests spiritual in nature. It is never acceptable to ask for a sign that might harm someone else in some way, or interfere with their free will. The Universe will not answer those requests, because it cannot by nature of its unconditional love for all things. You will simply not get your sign, but worse, you will send a very negative message to the Universe, which will come back to you tenfold. Be careful!

Once you have decided what it is you truly want, and your intention is positive and loving, you may proceed to construct your request.

Asking for Your Sign

The way you phrase your request is extremely important, because you must always send a clear message if you wish a clear answer. You will notice that we make requests in the form of declarative statements rather than questions. As with affirmations, these sentences are very powerful because they are direct and to the point. Many people with whom I have worked have had a difficult time creating these requests because they want too many things at once. You must be patient and understand that all things will come to you in their right and perfect time, so do not get anxious when doing sign work. Rather, take the time to develop specific requests and cultivate the patience to wait for the answers.

It is now time to get to the details of our task. Once you have decided what it is you want, you should sit down with a pen and paper and begin brainstorming different ways to ask for your sign.

When asking for a sacred sign you must phrase the request so that a "yes" or "no" answer is the result. There are other interpretations of signs and I will address them in later chapters, but for our purposes now, we must ask for the simplest of answers. A "yes" or "no" answer is both simple and powerful. Here is an example of a poorly worded request:

Should I buy a new car?

It does appear that this question is asking for a "yes" or "no" response, but it is not clear to the Universe. How will you know by the demonstration of a sign whether the answer is "yes" or "no"? You will need to *specify* what you will *accept* as a "yes" or "no." You are ultimately in control of this situation and you get to decide what the positive and negative indicators might be. If you do not indicate them, it will be difficult to interpret the answer. Therefore, you must guide the Universe to your specific understanding. Let us say that you have asked the above question as is. It will be answered because all requests are, but in a roundabout way. Your current vehicle might suddenly break down, you will receive a flyer in the mail, or a relative may ask if you wish to buy his car. All of these may be valid signs, but you will have to do some work to recognize them. Once you get good at this you will interpret such signs easily, but until then it is better and more efficient to form the request more specifically. Here is the statement reconstructed in a more effective manner:

Show me a sign that it is harmonious for me to buy a new car.

This request now asks for a "yes" answer and the implication here is that if a sign does not appear the answer is "no." I have found this method to be the most accurate. It does require that you *trust* that if you do not receive the sign, you will still accept that you have gotten your answer. There is no need to ask repeatedly. You will continue to get the same result! That is why trusting is such an important part of this process. It is also effective to put a *time limit* on the appearance of a sign so that if the answer is "no" you are not waiting indefinitely! I choose to give the Universe twenty-four hours to get the sign to me, because I feel that is realistic. It in no way should imply that you have to wait the full twenty-four hours to receive the sign. It could come to you within minutes. This is simply a range of time that I am most comfortable with, and have found to be most effective. I am more aware, and tend to pay closer attention to the appearance of the sign if I have more time to observe. When it finally appears, it is a delightful experience. It is also important to give the Universe a chance to get the sign to you. The more complicated the sign, the longer it takes to manifest. The Universe has to work through people and events in our real world to get the sign to us, so allowing for that is the best course of action. The better reconstruction of this statement is the following:

Within twenty-four hours, show me a sign that it is harmonious for me to buy a new car.

Now we have covered all the possibilities for error. We have made a powerful statement, and been specific as to what answer we wish to receive and when we wish to receive it. With this method, you cannot go wrong.

When "Yes" or "No" Is Not Enough

It is possible for us to be even more precise when asking for sacred signs. We may actually ask for a specific and personal sign to manifest. Earlier, I told you of the pennies I often ask to receive as a positive sign that all will be well in whatever situation I am considering. I have also asked for other specific signs as well. I have asked for all types of currency to appear, and they always do, not necessarily in their common form. Once I asked for a dollar bill as a sign that my finances would finally stabilize, and the next day, a friend gave me a bookmark in the form of a laminated, fake dollar bill. The sign will appear in some form, so be aware and notice how it manifests.

Ask for Clarity

Interpreting signs is a difficult job for both the novice and experienced seeker alike, so I have found it very helpful to ask for a clear and unmistakable sign to appear. When you ask for clarity, your job of interpreting the sign becomes easy. The sign will be obvious and you will not have to work too hard at interpretation. Unfortunately, some people still have trouble understanding their signs even after requesting clarity. I will help those of you who have that problem in chapter 5.

Whether you ask for a specific or general sign, for precise timing, or for clarity, your job has only begun. Truly understanding your sign will take practice, and the remaining two keys, Accept and Trust, will complete the process for you. So let us get to the task of writing those statements. It is important to literally write your statements on paper when you begin doing this work. It will help you to focus your attention, and come face-to-face with your needs, wants, and priorities.

Sacred Sign Statements

To assist you in forming your sacred requests, I have constructed the following statements. They consist of a specific request, and a declaration of gratitude to God/Universe, who is the source of the sign and your spiritual guidance. We would be extremely remiss if we did not recognize our Source with the utmost gratitude in doing all of our spiritual work. Take extra care to include the element of gratitude. At the conclusion of the gratitude statement is the phrase, "And so it is." This phrase assumes that we believe that what we have asked for will undoubtedly come into our life. This ending further reinforces our conviction and belief in the process.

Now you may take a few moments to fill in the remainder of the sacred statements with your specific desires. Form your statements on the lines below or in the sacred sign journal at the back of this book.

Requesting General Signs

"Send me a sign that I am supposed to _move to florida_. For this, I give thanks to you, God/Goddess/Spirit/Universe. And so it is!"

"Send me a sign that I am not supposed to _Contact or reconcile_. For this, I give thanks to you, God/Goddess/Spirit/Universe. And so it is!"

"Show me a sign that it is harmonious for me to _buy a house in CA_ For this, I give thanks to you, God/Goddess/Spirit/Universe. And so it is!"

"Show me a sign that it is not harmonious for me to _leave CA_. For this, I give thanks to you, God/Goddess/Spirit/Universe. And so it is!"

"Give me a sign that I should _stay in CA_. For this, I give thanks to you, God/Goddess/Spirit/Universe. And so it is!"

"Give me a sign that I should not _Contact ~~Joe~~_. For this, I give thanks to you, God/Goddess/Spirit/Universe. And so it is!"

Requesting Specific Signs

"Show me a sign in the form of _stranger (man) saying hi to me_, that it is harmonious (not harmonious) for me to _meet my future hubby_. For this, I give thanks to you, God/Goddess/Spirit/Universe. And so it is!"

"If a _____ appears in my life in any form, I trust that it is a clear sign from God/Goddess/Spirit/Universe that I should (should not)_____ _____. For this, I give thanks to you, God/Goddess/Spirit/Universe. And so it is!"

Adding Timing to a General Sign

"Within twenty-four hours (one day, thirty-six hours, forty-eight hours, one week, etc.), show me a sign that (I am supposed to, not supposed to, it is harmonious for

me to, not harmonious for me to) _meet my future_ husband . For this,
I give thanks to you, God/Goddess/Spirit/Universe. And so it is!"

Adding Timing to a Specific Sign

"Within twenty-four hours (thirty-six hours, forty-eight hours, one week, etc.), show
me a sign in the form of _a pretty butterfly_, that it is harmonious (not harmonious) for me to _meet my future_ For this, I give thanks to you, God/
Goddess/Spirit/Universe. And so it is! _it is_

"If a _butterfly_ appears in my life within twenty-four hours , (thirty-six
hours, forty-eight hours, one week, etc.), in any form, I trust that it is a clear sign
from God/Goddess/Spirit/Universe that I should (should not) _stay
in CA_. For this, I give thanks to you, God/Goddess/Spirit/Universe. And so it is!"

In forming your request you may use whatever language is comfortable for you,
or just use the examples above. They will work!

Focusing Your Energy

Working with sacred signs is most effective when we focus our energy. In my experience, the best way to do that is through ritual. We benefit by creating a personal ritual to do spiritual work in many more ways than are obvious. In taking the time to
communicate with Spirit in a structured way, we establish a constant in our lives,
something to look forward to. A personalized ritual generates a feeling of connect-
edness to God, and is a very tangible way for us to participate actively in the creation
of the future of our lives. Ritual puts us in touch with our Creator in a very intimate
setting and is a special event we share that is uniquely ours. Rituals may be used for
any request or need we may have. The Sacred Sign Ritual is simple and to the point,
and does not require any elaborate tools. It will not take very long to do, and is
enjoyable.

Planning your ritual before you set out to perform it is important. Finding a
place to carry it out is of primary importance. You should always perform your ritual when you are alone, or in an undisturbed area. You will need a surface that will
serve as your altar upon which to place a candle, or any other sacred objects you

choose to use to enhance your work. A dresser in a bedroom will suffice, or a small table or nightstand. Even a sturdy box turned upside down and covered with a lovely cloth will work. Use your imagination.

The tools are simple. A single candle, preferably white, will work. White is a neutral color and will not distract or influence your intention in any way. Using a candle in sign work is different from using it in other manifesting rituals, because you simply need it as a point of focus and relaxation, rather than an energy source to help in the manifesting process. An unbreakable candleholder should be used, preferably metal—glass could overheat and explode. Believe me, I have done this! The candle itself may be a taper or votive, whichever you prefer.

If you wish, you may complement your ritual with crystals, stones, spiritual statues, or icons that connect you to the Divine. None of these are required in asking for sacred signs. Just the focused intention is enough to send the request to the Universe. We use these helpmates for our own personal enhancement, and to further focus our energy.

A visualization meditation should always be included within the ritual. You may use the sacred sign meditation included at the end of this chapter, or create one of your own that you record in the journal. Meditation calms the mind, removes conflicting thoughts, and reaffirms our intention. It strengthens the request by further focusing your energy. The pictures and images you form in your mind help to change those outmoded concepts imbedded in your subconscious that might block your success. The constructive images replace thoughts of doubt and failure. Your brain will not process both positive and negative emotions simultaneously. Just try to laugh and cry at the same time. One of the two always dominates. Your meditation provides the peace of mind and reassurance that you are one with Spirit, and removes stress. The added benefit is the relaxed feeling in both mind and body you may carry throughout your day!

Here is a checklist of the simple steps you must take prior to beginning the ritual.

- Write your sacred sign request.

- Choose a meditation.

- Decide upon a time of day and a private space in your home to enact your ritual.

- Choose the candle, tools, and surface (altar) you wish to use and arrange it as you wish.

- Turn off the telephone or any other device that might distract you.

- If you live with pets, put them in another room.

- Ask others who live with you to give you this alone-time. (You need your full attention and complete concentration when you perform this ritual.)

Once you have completed the preliminary tasks you are ready to begin the Sacred Sign Ritual. The one I recommend follows. To make it more your own, add any elements of your choice that represent your spiritual commitment, or just use it as is.

The Sacred Sign Ritual

1. Go to your ritual space and dim the lights.

2. Sit or kneel in front of your altar.

3. Light the candle.

4. Read your sacred sign statement of request aloud, and then place the paper in front of the candle.

5. Enter into your sacred sign meditation and visualization by taking three gentle breaths and focusing upon your request. After the meditation, continue to breathe normally, and imagine that you have already received your sign and are content with that knowledge. Feel satisfied knowing you will finally take action that is divinely guided and cannot be wrong. Remain in this state of peace and tranquility for a few moments, knowing that your request was heard by the Universe/God/Goddess/Spirit, and will be answered.

6. When you are totally at peace with your request, and when you are ready, take three gentle breaths, inhaling joy and contentment, and exhaling any doubt or fear.

7. Take a final breath, inhaling peace and light, and as you exhale, return to full consciousness relaxed and refreshed, and open your eyes.

That is it. Now patiently and peacefully wait for your sacred sign to enter your world!

Questions?

There are always questions about asking for signs and the ritual involved. Those asked most often follow, with what I hope are comforting answers.

- May I include the name of someone in the sacred sign statement?

- May I ask for more than one sign at once?

- When is it appropriate to ask for another, different sign?

- How long will the ritual take?

- Do I need to repeat the ritual often?

- Do I have to write my sacred sign statement down every time I do the ritual?

- May I perform multiple rituals on the same day?

Let us address each of these very important questions.

May I include the name of someone in the sacred sign statement?

It is generally not good policy to include someone else's name in the ritual. We always need to take care not to try to manipulate anyone's free will. It is safer not to name anyone else in your sign request, even if it seems appropriate. For example, if you are asking for a sign that you will marry your boyfriend, instead of saying, "Show me a sign that I will marry Harry," it is better to say, "Show me a sign that I will be happily married." The second statement removes any possibility of an inadvertent manipulation of Harry's free will. Working with Spirit is not an exact science, but it should never harm anyone, and we must make every effort to respect the free will of others.

There is a circumstance, though, in which you may mention someone's name. When you are requesting information that will be in the highest good of that person, mentioning their name or title will be harmless. As stated earlier, when my father was ill I asked for a sign that he would live, and my first beautiful penny appeared. I had said specifically, "Give me a sign that Dad will live." Within minutes, I spotted that mysterious penny. Because I was asking in his highest good, I was not attempting to manipulate Dad in any way. I was simply asking for information. The Universe chose to give that information to me, at that time. There is a difference between requesting information and possible manipulation.

Getting back to Harry, if you really, really want to marry him and name him in your request, you take the chance of influencing his higher consciousness on an unseen level. You also limit your own future. If Harry is all wrong for you and you have somehow gotten him to agree to marry you, years later, you might become miserable with him. Had you simply requested whether or not you would be married, you open the door to your perfect mate, should Harry turn out to be Mr. Wrong! Isn't it better to know you will be happily married, whether it is to Harry or not?

May I ask for more than one sign at once?

Do not ask for more than one sign at once. It scatters your energy and disrupts your focus. As you know, focus is very important to receiving your answers. Do not clutter your sacred sign statement with several requests like, "Give me a sign that I will be happily married, have a baby, and get the job of my dreams." Wow! The only message you are sending is one of confusion. *Make only one request per statement.*

When is it appropriate to ask for another, different sign?

Wait until your sign appears, or your personal time limit is up if you have included one, before asking for another, different sign.

How long will the ritual take?

Your ritual may take as much time as you wish to devote to it. I have found that a simple five-minute ritual is just as effective as a lengthy one. There is no required amount of time, but you should follow the steps faithfully for best results.

Do I need to repeat the ritual often?

There is generally no need to repeat the ritual for the same sign request. You are not paying attention if you are not aware of the answer! Rest assured that Spirit has registered your request, and answered it.

Do I have to write my sacred sign statement down every time I do the ritual?

You should write your statement only once for each sign you are requesting. When one is answered, write the statement for the next one, and so on. You need a new one for each request.

May I perform multiple rituals on the same day?

Again, scattered energy results when you try to ask for too much on the same day. You may, if your sign appears within minutes. It is a wonderful gift but less common. I still suggest waiting a day before your next request. Enjoy the moment!

Focus Further

This next exercise is designed to help you synthesize all you have learned in this chapter on the first key—Ask. It will assist you in forming your sacred sign statements, and deciding upon which type of sign to ask for.

Exercise #6

Answer the following questions honestly, and follow any additional instructions to the best of your ability. As always, you may record your answers here or in the sacred sign journal.

1. What do you really want to happen to solve your problem? Or, what is the outcome you are seeking for your dilemma or situation in question?

Should I move out of CA? Will I ever marry someone here?

2. Why are you seeking divine guidance in the form of a sacred sign?

I need some type of confirmation to what my higher self already knows.

3. Before using signs, how did you receive your messages from God/Goddess/Universe/Spirit?

An innate knowing radiomancy from song phrase on TV or radio

4. Are you absolutely prepared to accept and follow the guidance you receive? Why or why not?

yes I am, signs are tools from God

5. Which do you think would serve your purpose best, a general or specific sign? Why?

A specific sign, its too easy to read into generalities Specific works best for me

6. Write your request now in both a general and a specific form.

Give me a sign in the form of a butterfly in the next 24 hours If Im to meet my soulmate here.

7. Would adding a timeframe be helpful? If so, add one to the above requests.

Yes, having that knowledge within 24 hours would be more concrete for me

8. On the lines that follow, indicate what tools you would like to use in your ritual.

my crystal ball, my scarab, a candle, & my Yogananda ritual thing

9. Create a personal meditation for your ritual.

Divine mother I'm asking you now for a sign, Jesus Christ, Kali & Yogananda guide me & show me the answers.

Analyze Your Answers

Question #1 forces you to deeply examine your motives in your difficult situation, and helps you to think about how you will respond, no matter what the result. This question should turn on some light bulbs in your head!

Questions #2 and #3 get you to take a look back at how you have handled your past situations spiritually. Looking at what you have done before helps you get a stronger sense of your personal spirituality, and how thinking this way has served you in the past.

Question #4 smacks you in the face with reality. You must commit to this work, be willing to accept your message, and do what it takes to follow the sacred advice you receive. If you had trouble answering this one, you may not be ready to do this sign work.

Questions #5 through #9 are the practical, hands-on entries that should be very helpful in organizing your thoughts and creating your personalized ritual. Have fun with them!

Key #1 Meditation

Ask

Find a comfortable position in your chair, hands on your lap, and feet flat on the floor. Close your eyes and take three gentle breaths, inhaling through the nose, and exhaling through the mouth. . . . Continue breathing gently with mouth closed. As you do, feel a wave of relaxation moving from the top of your head, slowly down, down, down, to the tip of your toes. . . . Breathe gently and repeat your sacred sign statement silently. . . . Tell the Universe/God/ Goddess/Spirit that you are open, willing, and ready to receive your sign, in an absolutely clear, kind, and loving way. . . . As you continue to breathe gently, inhale peace and tranquility and exhale all doubt and fear. Relax in the knowledge that your sacred sign is on its way. . . . After a few moments, and when you are ready, take another gentle breath, and as you exhale, return to full consciousness and open your eyes.

If you wish, you may record your response to this meditation in the sacred sign journal at the back of this book.

Key #1 Affirmation

Ask

"I am open, ready, and willing to receive this sacred sign in my highest and greatest good, and that of all concerned. The sacred sign comes to me now in a kind and loving way, and is completely clear and understandable. For this I give thanks. And so it is!"

Important Points to Remember

- The three Mistake-Proof Keys to the Knowledge of the Universe are:

    Ask

    Accept

    Trust

- In order to work with the keys effectively we must agree to eliminate fear.

- In working with signs you must know what you want.

- You must have clear intentions.·

- When you ask for a sign, you must be prepared to follow through with action.

- Signs are best at answering "yes—no" questions.

- To make sure your sign is understandable, remember to ask for clarity.

- Use a set form to ask for general or specific signs, and be consistent.

- You may add timing to a request.

- Your energy must always remain focused.

- Use the sacred sign ritual, or a personally designed ritual, to enhance your sign request.

- A meditation and vivid visualization may be used for further focus.

- It is generally better to not include someone's name in a sign request to avoid spiritual manipulation.

- Do not ask for more than one sign at once.

- Wait until your sign appears before asking for another, different one.

- There is no need to repeat the ritual for the same sign request.

- Write your sacred sign statement only once for each sign you request.

- Wait a day before performing another or different ritual.

Chapter Five

Key #2—Accept: How to Recognize and Interpret Your Message

Acceptance is one of the more difficult keys to master. When asking for a sacred sign, you have to be at peace with whatever answer you receive, even if it is not the one you hoped for. Using the example given previously, let us say you wish to know if the timing is right to buy a car, and you really want a new car. If the sign indicates that the timing is favorable for such a purchase, you would be comfortable following that guidance because it is what you really want. Should the sign indicate that the timing is not right, then alternately, you should be willing to accept and follow that guidance as well. When you pursue sacred sign work, you are telling the Universe that you will agree to accept and follow the advice given. If you do not like the answer you got, asking for another sign on the same subject will not help. You will just get the same answer. To avoid frustration, listen to the message the first time it is given. It surely saves lots of time and effort, not to mention helping to avoid emotional angst.

But acceptance does not come easily to us when we are attached to the answer we truly want to receive. As Dr. Deepak Chopra tells us in many of his books, we must practice "detachment" from results. Meaning, we should try to keep a cool distance and not get overly emotional about the message we receive. We must be neutral in accepting the answers from the Universe. This keeps us balanced and in flow. Staying neutral requires a belief in the axiom, "Everything happens for a reason." If you can approach the divine guidance you get with that perspective in mind, you will be less likely to be disturbed by the message, and will be able to view it objectively.

Besides taking an objective viewpoint, acceptance of sign messages requires that we make our personal peace with the answer we received, and not make too many attempts to maneuver the Universe into giving us the answer we want. Such attempts will be futile. Believe me. I have tried! The more accepting you become, the more in flow you are, and you will be calm enough to understand why you received the answer you did, without concern or worry.

There are practical methods to help us work with this key successfully. In this chapter, you will learn how to recognize and interpret your message from the Universe, as promised. I have broken down my method for you into four elements or stages of development. The first will help you to identify your sacred sign when it comes to you. The second will assist you in interpreting it to your best understanding. The third will teach you how to send a message of acknowledgement and thanks to Spirit for the answer to your request. The fourth will help you to find the courage to act upon the message.

Stage I: Recognizing Your Sacred Sign

Recognizing your sign is not as difficult as you may think. It requires awareness. You must become aware and look for your sign as it manifests in your life. Once you have asked for it, you must then be in a heightened state of awareness until the sign appears. There is nothing special or difficult to do to become aware. You must simply tell yourself that you will be sensitive to your environment until the sign appears, by being observant. For instance, if you have asked for a sign within twenty-four hours, then for that twenty-four-hour period you must be extremely perceptive. Pay attention to what is happening around you. The sign may appear clearly and obviously, or in a strange way, which will require some thinking and interpreting on your part. Whatever the delivery system, you must be ready to receive it. What follows are all of the ways I know to become aware of and recognize your sacred sign when it appears. Study them carefully and commit them to memory. When you do, you will not have a problem recognizing your messages from the Universe.

- Stay alert when something different happens in your life that is not part of your daily routine. Register what is happening, make a note of it on paper if necessary, but do not write it off as odd or coincidental.

- Actively look for your sign in ordinary places. Your sign might show up as a title or line from a book or magazine, or the actual book itself will be the sign, just as I encountered the day that I first met my guide, Roger! Little did I know that my attempt to return a book to its proper place on the shelf would lead to a life-changing sign, hidden in a simple experience.

- Music is another vehicle for signs. Many people will hear a song and recognize either a title or line from that song that appears to answer their request. When you have asked for a sign, start paying closer attention to music whether it comes to you on the radio, on television, piped into a store as you shop, on a friends' stereo playing when you visit, from a nightclub band, in the dentist's or doctor's office, etc. You get the idea. One of my clients often receives her signs while driving in her car. Whenever she needs assistance, she asks for it and invariably gets her answer in a familiar tune or lyric line. It serves as a great source of comfort to her. And it may well be your primary way of receiving signs as well. Time and practice will reveal if that is true for you.

- Watch television and movies with a new eye toward receiving and recognizing your signs. Sometimes an actor, line of dialogue, television commercial, or show title may apply to your sign request. You may even build it into your sacred sign statement—for example, "If it is harmonious for me to pursue a music career, Frank Sinatra will appear on TV or in a movie within twenty-four hours." This is an unusual request since he is deceased, so if he shows up within twenty-four hours, pay attention!

- Actual material objects you specify may appear as your sign. They are the easiest to recognize, such as the pennies I request and inevitably find. Over time, you will see if this form of manifesting is working for you, too.

- An unexpected event or chance meeting may be your sign. You might be anywhere at all and run into someone you haven't seen for some time, and realize that is your sign. One of my clients asked for a sign as to whether she should marry her boyfriend, and the next day, she just happened to run into her ex-husband, whom she hadn't seen in years! What do you think the sign meant?

- The most personal way signs appear is through your intuition, which is defined as sudden strong feelings, urges, or a sense of knowingness. I am talking about anything from a craving for pizza, to an inner prompting to go somewhere you did not intend to go. One of my clients met her husband this way. She was working as a waitress in a pizza parlor and her future mate just happened to have a craving for a pepperoni pizza so he stopped in. He said he had asked for a sign that a wonderful woman would come into his life, and that evening, when he found his favorite Chinese restaurant was closed, he had a "feeling" that he should go to this specific pizzeria. The rest is history!

  After asking for a sign, I have found myself feeling the need to drive to a particular store when my intention was to go elsewhere. I am not ever sure why I should go there, but I am aware of and always follow the urging of my intuition. I recall that one of my signs was waiting in a store for me. The request I made was for a sign that it would be harmonious to change careers. I was the director of a nonprofit teen organization at the time, but my heart was in the theatre. Up to this point, I was concerned that I would not be able to make a living performing, so I was hesitant to leave my secure position. A few days later, my intention was to go to the grocery store, but I followed my intuition to a department store, with no goal to buy anything, when I ran into an old friend who had just been cast in a play that needed an actress, and he thought I would be perfect for the role. There was my sign. I made the change and it paid off in a stint Off-Broadway!

  Pay close attention to your intuition in recognizing your sign. It may come in that very subtle way.

- Sacred signs may come to you through life circumstances surrounding a personal incident. One of my friends wanted to find a special school program for her young son. Two opportunities presented themselves and she was not sure which would be more beneficial to him, so she asked for a sign. She and her husband had an appointment with the officials at one of the schools. She felt she had not received her sign yet, so they decided to go for the interview anyway. She, her husband, and their son set out for the meeting, and the boy needed a restroom break, as children often do. The closest place to stop was the restaurant they owned, which was closed that day. When they shut the door to leave, they suddenly realized they had locked all their keys inside, car keys and all! They were completely unable to call to cancel, or even drive to the appointment. My client was convinced that was her sign, and this was not the program for her son. She is currently pursuing the alternate program, which seems right and perfect for him.

- Surprising events, extremely positive or negative, may also be signs. Joyful encounters, receiving a gift, or an unexpected telephone call might all be messages from the Universe in response to your requests. Do not discount anything after asking for your sign. Remember, the messages may reach you using your own environment as the instrument of wisdom.

- You might receive your sign through spiritual or paranormal means. If you are a spiritual seeker, this method is very comfortable for you. Dreams may be the messengers of your sign, and you may even ask specifically that your sign come in dreams if you wish! You might receive messages through intuitive counselors, psychics, or mediums, from spirit entities, loved ones who have passed, spirit guides, or angels.

As you can see, recognizing your signs requires a unique awareness of your world, your surroundings, people, spiritual vibrations, and your intuition. With time and attention, you will find recognizing your signs an easy and very rewarding experience. It is not enough just to recognize the obvious signs as they appear. You must make sense out of those that are less obvious, such as signs involving circumstances, event/personal incidents, and dreams.

Let us move on to solve that dilemma in the next stage, which will help you to interpret your sacred signs.

Stage II: Interpreting Your Sacred Sign

Understanding and interpreting a sign may be difficult for most people if the sign does not come in the way they had expected. Should it come in literal form, such as a specific object, person, or event, interpreting it is an easy task. If you ask for a rose as a sign and someone literally hands you a rose, no interpretation is necessary. However, if a sign takes on symbolic form, things might get a bit complicated. You must work to relate the sign to the intention behind the request.

Literal signs and those that require interpretation come to us equally. We cannot control the delivery method. God gets to handle that. Nevertheless, there are measures we may take to clarify them, so do not be discouraged, and remain aware.

To assist you with your more complicated sacred signs there are two tools to help with interpreting them. They are as follows:

- Use logic and reason.

- Use your intuition.

Using the Tools

A sign might be hard to understand because we do not always recognize its pattern as it manifests in our life. In this case, our logic becomes a handy tool. To see the patterns, we must use our powers of logic and reason. That means after asking for a sign, we must attempt to *figure out what relationship* certain incidents have to each other as they begin to occur in our lives. We must determine how the unfolding events relate to our request. Then we may determine whether or not they constitute a sign.

Along with logic and reason, we should use our inner promptings, commonly called our intuition. Sign interpretation is the one case in which these elements work together harmoniously. I have often been known to discourage the use of logic and reason in making life decisions, in favor of using intuition. But when it comes to signs, your intuition can and will be confirmed by adding the power of reason to your interpretation. Let us look at how these elements can clear up the confusion in interpreting our signs.

Interpreting Circumstance Signs

A circumstance is defined as a condition or state through which a sign appears. In other words, certain conditions exist surrounding the delivery of the sign. For example, if you ask for a sign that it is a good time to buy a car, and then receive a flyer in the mail advertising a sale on the very car you want, a delivery condition exists there. There are conditions evident, such as the advertiser, printer, and post office, that exist in getting the sign to you. Understanding and interpreting these circumstances will require you to first: allow your intuition to speak to you; and second: to use reasoning to interpret and accept the circumstances as the sign.

In order to tap into your intuition, when you first suspect that a sign is revealing itself through circumstances in your life, you should quiet your mind, close your eyes for a moment, and go into a simple breathing meditation. After taking three gentle breaths, put the idea of the sign into your mind and notice whether you feel confident or doubtful. Confidence signals that your spirit believes a sign is coming. Doubt indicates the opposite. If you feel that your intuition is telling you to pursue the circumstances with further awareness and thought, use logic to interpret it. Consider the odds of such a circumstance happening either within the timeframe of your sign, or at all. In the above example, it is no coincidence that you receive a flyer within twenty-four hours of asking for a sign. A doubter would call it coincidence, but a believer would see how spiritually logical that is! Use your logic in this way to complement your intuition. It will help you to conclude that you have received a sign.

Another way to interpret your message and presume that you have received your sign is to consider the complications involved in that so-called "coincidence." The Universe had to go through a lot of trouble and depend upon the free wills of many people to get that car flyer to you. Just think about that. Someone had to think of having a sale, design the flyer, print it, distribute it, mail it, and deliver it to your mailbox! What are the odds? This pattern clearly demonstrated Carl Jung's theory of synchronicity. Here we see a series of circumstances that seem to be coincidental, but bear a meaningful result. If you learn to approach the interpretation of a sign in this way, using intuition first and logic second, you will be astounded at the power and order behind the message, and the tremendous gift that it is!

Interpreting Event/Personal Incident Signs

An event or personal incident may be a sign that also needs the help of our intuition, logic, and reasoning to interpret. An event/personal incident is defined as an occurrence that happens, seemingly unbeknown to an individual, and apart from their control. An event feels as if something is happening that is completely out of our hands. Your intuition will tell you whether the event is meaningful or not. If your intuition seems to be telling you to use logic, now is the time to shift into think-mode.

One of my clients had an altercation with a close friend, seemingly unprovoked by her. She was so upset and wondered why her friend had suddenly turned on her. A few weeks later, another friend did the same. After the second incident, her intuition told her that something significant was happening. In thinking about the situation, she realized that she was in receipt of a sign. Through logic and reasoning she concluded that loyal friends would not mistreat her in such a hurtful way, and that those folks were not really her friends at all. Guidance was sent to her to reevaluate her friendships, and let them go, if necessary. In a sense, the Universe/God was protecting her through the sign, helping her to make a decision as to how to handle a very disturbing situation, and make her personal peace with it. She paid attention to the promptings of her intuition and used her thoughts to find clarity.

This event, the betrayal of her friends, seemed to occur outside of my client's control, yet, as metaphysicians, we believe that all things result from the need of our soul to grow in enlightenment. In essence, she attracted the sign, because her soul needed to learn a valuable lesson about friendship.

When an event occurs in your life that seems totally unwarranted, and takes you by surprise, use your intuition, reason and logic to see what the guidance truly is. It will take some time, because we must first move beyond the emotion of the moment, and shift our minds past the pain, to the real message. Removing from, or moving through, the emotion is a wonderful way to calm your heart and accept the more difficult circumstances life presents.

Interpreting Dream Signs

Dreams are a fascinating subject for many of us, and they, too, may be the harbingers of sacred signs. We might have a dream and then receive the sign shortly thereafter, or the dream itself might be the sign. Dreams are difficult enough to interpret in their own right, without trying to determine if they portend the arrival of a sign. Yet, if we observe them closely, we might find the sign easier to understand when it does manifest. Again, intuition, logic, and reasoning are the handy tools in identifying our divine messages.

In chapter 2, I described a series of dreams experienced by my student, Garth, concerning his future career pursuits. His intuition told him that this decision was very important and that he needed divine assistance. He then asked for a sign to come in his dreamtime and it did, guiding him to choose, through logic and reasoning, between one possible career or another.

If the dream seems too bizarre and filled with contradictions, it is safe to say that it is not a message concerning a sign. If it were, it would be more clear and specific to your needs, such as Garth's career dream. If you were requesting a sign to assist in a marriage decision, you might dream about your future spouse, or a wedding, or see yourself cohabiting, etc. That would be clear, but if you see yourself and your fiancé in a rocket ship going to Mars, you are probably not getting a sign. Use your intuition to determine whether the dream seems to be one containing a sign, and then go from there.

So you see, interpreting signs is not as difficult as it appears to be if you approach systematically using the sacred power of inner knowing along with the brainpower of the mind. However, your work is not done yet! Once you have recognized and interpreted your sacred sign, you must tell the Universe that you truly accept it by acknowledging it.

Acknowledging Your Sacred Sign

Once a sign manifests into our world we have the tendency to discount it or question its validity. We sometimes do that even after we have interpreted it and agreed that it truly *might* be a sign! I am always amazed at how many people tend to allow their doubts to interfere with their sacred messages. If you tend to waver a bit, you should work at resisting and eliminating doubt by saying this affirmation:

"I accept my sacred sign now. And so it is!"

This simple prayer will help clear out any second thoughts you might have. Say it as often as necessary.

When you acknowledge your sign, you send a message of complete acceptance to Spirit. You must admit to it, concede to it, and agree to it. Rather than attributing it to luck, you must send the message back to God/Goddess/Universe that you believe you have been blessed with guidance. Quite plainly, you must express gratitude.

Gratitude is very powerful because saying "thank you" when you perceive your sign sends a clear message of acceptance to the Universe, who in turn, gives you back more reasons to be grateful. In other words, your signs will continue to come more easily and clearly when you notify God/Goddess that you are ready, willing, and able to trust in its guidance. Wow! What a payoff, and one we cannot afford to miss in doing our sign work.

We have already given thanks in advance when we wrote our sacred sign statements, but it is important to reinforce that gesture after the sign appears, as well. Here is a simple affirmation you might use to send that positive message of thanks:

> *"Thank you, God/Goddess/Spirit/Universe for this sacred sign, and for all that are yet to come. And so it is!"*

Remember to give thanks before and after your sign appears.

Acting upon the Message

It is not enough to ask for a sign. In order to benefit from the message of the sign, you must make a decision to act on the guidance in some way. It makes sense that if we ask for an either-or answer we are willing to act one way or the other upon the message the sign delivers. If the answer to your request is "no," then not acting, or finding an alternative action, completes the sequence. For example, let us go back to the car decision. If your sign indicates that it would indeed be harmonious for you to purchase a new car, which is a "yes" answer, then by all means whip out that checkbook and have fun! If your sign indicates that it would not be harmonious for you to purchase a new car, which is a "no" answer, then an equal alternative action is required to complete the cycle. Therefore, you would not buy the car, but, alternately, you would repair the one you already have, or pursue the purchase of a *used* car, asking for a sign that the new action is harmonious. Be systematic in your approach, and you will have no trouble using signs to help make major decisions.

Sometimes taking an alternate action is painful. When you get a sign that indicates you should not marry your sweetie, what should you do? Postpone the nuptials, because the sign might indicate that the timing is just not harmonious now. It is not necessarily discounting a future wedding. That is still a possibility. Never take drastic action in response to a sign. Do not tell your Romeo that you cannot marry him. Just tell him the timing is off, and promise to talk about it in the future. Then in a few months, ask for a sign again. If you continue to get a "no" sign after repeated requests, turn to your intuition for the answer. Are you just not willing to accept it? Are you refusing to see that he is not the one for you, and ignoring what you might know in your heart to be true? Soul search and the answer will become clear.

Take the appropriate action, or enact an alternative and you cannot go wrong. If you do nothing, you send a message back to the Universe that you do not trust the guidance, and you will have great difficulty interpreting and even receiving signs in the future. Remember, the Universe sends back to us tenfold what we send to it. There is that pesky Law of Circulation again! You have been warned.

Exercise #7

Here is an exercise designed to help you recognize and interpret your sacred signs, by building the powers of observation and awareness. Answer the following four questions and record your answers here or in the Sacred Sign Journal.

1. Take a few moments and gaze out the nearest window. As you do, make a mental note of all that you see. Now without looking back, record as many details as you have observed.

Andrews like, pepperwood tree melissas apt, sunshine weather blue sky

2. What are your passions? Do you love music, art, books, sports? List the recreational pursuits you love most, and recall any "coincidences" that have resulted through them. (This might take a while!)

Art, self-help books, exercising, dining & conversing with friends, swap meet, going to vegas, visiting family & friends

3. Are your dreams vivid? Do you often feel that they are trying to tell you something? Record your latest, most vivid dream, and describe what you feel it was trying to tell you.

dreams very vivid Jim's house was pitch black inside – showing me our relationship is dead

4. Imagine that you have asked for a sign indicating that it would be harmonious for you to pursue a new career. In the next few days, you chat with a colleague at work who tells you he is disgruntled with his career, a friend offers to help you rewrite your resume, and you hear a song on the radio with the catchy title, "Change Your Mind, Change Your Life." Did you get your sign? If so, what was it and the message it was sending?

its an absolutie, go ahead to forge forward in a new career

Question #1 tests the power of simple observation. Were you able to remember what you saw out the window easily? If not, you need to spend a little time really appreciating what is happening around you. You could be missing your signs because you are just not paying attention!

Question #2 is designed to help you zero in on the most comfortable ways in which your psyche might receive signs. Some of us are more musical than others and pay closer attention to song lyrics and titles. The same is true of avid readers, sportsmen, artists, theatre buffs, etc. If you think hard enough you will recall a synchronistic event that occurred in your life through this particular channel, because Spirit already knows how to communicate with you. You just need to cooperate by becoming aware of your most powerful medium. It is highly likely that you have been receiving divine messages through one of these avenues all along, and not even realizing it.

Question #3 deals with dreams, which are one of the more common ways we may receive our sacred signs. Really analyze the dream you have recorded with a special focus upon how you felt while you were dreaming. If you felt joyful, the sign would be telling you to pursue your request. If not, it might be telling you that you should find an alternative. Feelings are as important as events in dreams, and can tell you a lot.

Question #4 is really a quiz to help you discern from outer circumstances whether you have received a sign or not. Without spoiling the surprise, I will tell you that there is a sign in that scenario, but I'll let you ponder the message it is conveying. Share it with others and see what they think.

Key #2 Meditation

Acceptance

Note: You must have already asked for a sign but not yet received an answer, before doing this meditation. You will see why.

Find a comfortable position in your chair, hands on your lap, and feet flat on the floor. Close your eyes and take three gentle breaths, inhaling through the nose, and exhaling through the mouth. . . . Continue breathing gently with mouth closed. As you do, feel a wave of relaxation moving from the top of your head, slowly down, down, down, to the tip of your toes. . . . Breathe gently and allow a mental picture to form of the events that might happen in your life if the guidance of your sign is "yes." Relax for a few moments. . . . Now, without stress or strain, see the opposite result happening and allow that picture to unfold. . . . Relax with that image for a few moments. . . . Remaining completely at peace, tell yourself you will be fine with either result. Tell the Universe/God/ Goddess/Spirit that you accept your sign, and are grateful for whatever the message might be. As you continue to breathe gently, inhale peace and tranquility and exhale all doubt and fear. Relax in the knowledge that you are divinely guided and therefore, all will be well. . . . After a few moments, and when you are ready, take another gentle breath, and as you exhale, return to full consciousness and open your eyes.

Key #2 Affirmation

Acceptance

"Thank you, God/Goddess/Spirit/Universe for this Sacred Sign. I receive it, welcome it, and accept it into my consciousness and my world, without doubt, fear, or judgment. I am in flow with life and acknowledge the divine presence within me. And so it is!"

Important Points to Remember

- When asking for a sacred sign you must accept whatever answer you receive.

- You must be willing to follow the divine guidance you are given.

- Do not ask for multiple signs if you do not like the message you receive.

- To recognize sacred signs, you must be in a heightened state of awareness.

- Pay attention to circumstances and what is happening around you.

- To be aware of and recognize your sacred signs, understand the following:

- Stay alert to new occurrences in your life.

- Look for your sign in ordinary places.

- Be open to the sign appearing through any number of vehicles.

- The arts, TV, radio, music may all be your sign.

- Material objects may appear as your sign.

- Signs appear through your intuition—feelings, urges, or knowingness.

- Signs may come through life circumstances surrounding a personal incident.

- Surprising events, positive or negative, may be signs.

- You may receive a sign through spiritual or paranormal means.

- It may be more difficult to recognize signs involving circumstances, event/ personal incidents, or dreams.

- A sign may not come in the way you expect.

- You must work to relate the sign to the intention behind the request.

- The two tools to help you interpret signs are logic/reason and your intuition.

- Once a sign appears we must acknowledge it with gratitude.

- We must act on the message we receive through our sign.

- The Universe will send back to us, tenfold, what we send to it.

Chapter Six

Key #3—Trust: How to Truly Believe

Now that you have mastered the first two keys, you'll need to use every ounce of personal conviction to master the third—Trust. Although we desperately want to believe that signs do occur and that the Universe is in constant contact with us through them, our human nature might cause us to question their validity at the core of our being. In our Western society, it is very easy to doubt things spiritual because we cannot see, hear, touch, taste, or smell them, even when they make themselves as obvious as possible. When you truly believe that you have received a sacred sign, all doubt vanishes and relief replaces fear. I tell my students, church members, and clients that in order to get the most mileage out of this type of sacred work, they must take three important steps: trust, believe, and surrender. If you can resolve to take those very important steps, you will find yourself rewarded by the Universe with immeasurable joy, abundance, and peace.

In this key, we will address each one of these objectives as they apply to sign work. Ultimately, your sign work will suffer, even if you do everything I've asked you to, if you do not trust that you deserve this gift from Spirit. Remember, you get back what you give. If you send the energy of distrust, you receive more reasons to be distrustful. You will end up finding fault with signs when they appear, and you will miss out on miraculous divine guidance.

Step #1: Trust

Logic may be your worst enemy when it comes to interpreting and believing in your sacred signs. Anyone who has done a considerable amount of spiritual work will tell you that reason and logic don't apply when negotiating with the Universe. This is so because, to Spirit, all things and energies exist simultaneously and are not subject to strict order. In other words, the Universe doesn't necessarily recognize time as an essential factor. What is more important to the Universe is intention, or our spiritual will behind our request. That's why you might make a request today, and receive the answer a year or two from now. Spirit just registers that you sincerely want something and trust that it will manifest into your life. A little thing like timing is incidental to God. You will always receive what you need precisely when you need it and not a moment sooner! It can be frustrating, so we try to nudge the Universe along a bit by setting our human time limits. When that is recognized, we see more immediate results. It's easy to trust when you get instant action, but much harder when the answer is, "You'll just have to wait a while." Then that old demon, logic, kicks in and we try desperately to justify why we want what we want now, not later. It is this process that is faulty, and might cause us to distrust the message the Universe is sending in response to our request.

Logically, when things appear in order, we feel satisfied. When events or circumstances do not appear to be in order and are more abstract, we begin to question. That is the case with most signs. They often do not appear in any order, or with any logic. How can one justify something that defies justification? Not an easy task! Therefore, we must fight the urge to shoot holes into our messages and train ourselves, if we are not so inclined, to trusting what does not seem logical. At the risk of sounding contradictory, let's look at the solution to this errant process logically, with some tools to help you stop doubting and start trusting.

- Do not question a sign with logic when it appears. Rather, look for the circumstances surrounding it, and how they might impact your request. If you ask for a sign that you should take that job offer, and you see a TV commercial made by that very company within the next few days, trust it! It is not a coincidence. It is a sign, as clear as day. Of course it's not logical, but it is just as powerful as logic when you consider it without skepticism.

- Should you not receive your sign immediately, it does not necessarily mean you won't get it at all. Try not to allow your doubt to defeat the sign work over time. Sometimes it takes the Universe time to reveal a message to you. Be patient. Ask again before you pooh-pooh the whole process.

- Fight the urge to call it all a waste of time if you do not receive the answer you want. Many of us just take the easy way out by declaring that the whole thing is a hoax simply because we didn't get our way. Instead, tell yourself that all things happen for a reason, and if your answer is not what you want, you will trust that the Universe knows the bigger picture, and something better is on the way.

- To trust your signs you must actively make parallels in your mind. You should observe how the answer came to you, and in what form. Then you should determine how it might apply to your life and particular situation. When you follow this method, logic becomes your friend, as a tool to assist you in trusting your messages.

- Use affirmations to remove doubt and enforce trust in your consciousness. Try saying, "I trust the Universe/Spirit/God/Goddess to always act in my highest good. And so it is!" Say it often enough to silence that little nagging voice in your head that has a tendency to say, "No it doesn't!" Believe me, when you say this affirmation often enough, you will feel tremendous peace of mind. Try it!

- Along with saying the affirmation, there is the necessity to make a personal and possibly earth-shaking vow, to believe in a power greater than your ego. For most of us, the idea that we cannot and should not attempt to control every aspect of our lives is just downright ridiculous. I'm telling you that you don't have to! Spirit is more than willing to guide each of us to our greatest life if we only ask, watch, and wait. We have to get a grip on that human side of our nature, and trust the God within us.

- Forget the past, and learn to trust yourself. Ah, ha! I'll bet you didn't expect this one! How can you trust in the Universe when you don't even trust yourself? How many times have you doubted your own ability to make good decisions, choices, or take good action in your life? I would venture to say, quite often. When we look back at our past and pick it apart piece-by-piece, judging our action, inaction, hurts, injustices, etc., we create an environment of distrust in ourselves. Forgive yourself, now, and know that Spirit has already done so.

- Whatever you do, do not doubt your inner voice. Instead, think of it as the voice of God within you, and pay attention to it. The feelings in your "gut" are valid and should always, always be trusted. Cultivate self-confidence in your choices and decisions, and know that they are divinely guided.

- Give yourself a break. Resist the urge to put yourself down. When a sign appears that might be difficult to understand, do not make yourself crazy second-guessing your interpretation of it. Do not feel stupid or unenlightened because you cannot figure it out immediately. Calm down, take a deep breath, and trust that you have received all the information you need to understand the message. Meditate on the sign, and ask Spirit for help in explaining it to you. You will receive your assistance. It is a matter of—you guessed it—trust!

- Expect the best. Tell yourself that you will receive a clear, understandable sign that will answer your deepest question, and provide you with the guidance you need. Do not entertain thoughts of anything less.

- Do not be afraid to be different, or think differently from others. Working with the Universe might be unusual, but that is only because we have not been schooled in this type of action. What is unusual is not necessarily wrong, odd, or weird. You know that to be true, so stop worrying about the consequences of straying beyond the norm. Trust that different is good!

- Know that each sign and its message is a unique cog in the wheel of life, each contributing to a greater whole. When you receive guidance for a particular situation you will see that, sooner or later, it applies to the entire scheme of your life. Do not get caught up in limited thinking. Embrace an unlimited view of your life.

- Allow yourself to be vulnerable. When you trust and turn your life over to a higher loving power, you become vulnerable in a good way. An attitude of trust tells Spirit that you wish to co-create your life, and you are confident that your highest good will result. Allow yourself to open to the wisdom of the Universe, without fear of being manipulated by what some might believe is an ominous force. God/Spirit would never force anyone to do anything! You have free will. It is all, always, up to you. Therefore, surrendering your need to God gets you immediate divine assistance. There is no greater help we could receive.

- Finally, and foremost, develop trust in the phrase, "With God all things are possible."

Step #2: Believe

Sacred sign work will change the way you think, because receiving signs is extremely encouraging. Receiving signs makes believers out of most of us. Believing is the next step to ultimately trusting the Universe. When you believe in an idea or concept, your logical mind becomes confident, and self-determination grows. Trust in people, situations, or what is happening around you, becomes an easy task, not fraught with doubt. Believing requires courage and dedication to a higher principle, beyond that of your everyday, conscious existence. Belief is powerful and your newfound power motivates you to live your life in a much more fulfilling way, just knowing that all will be well as you live with right intention. It embraces that which we cannot see, or perceive with our senses. Belief is God in action in our lives. It is faith, conviction, principle, and idea. Let's examine at each of these.

- Faith, as I define it, is not the traditional view that is familiar to us all. That kind of faith implies religiosity, or a belief in a particular doctrine or system. A new concept of faith, and the one that I teach, embodies a renewed confidence in oneself and our ability to tap into the force that created us all. It accepts that we are one with our Source, Spirit, and together we can form a loving, joyful, abundant life. There is no doubt, fear, or questioning where this faith is concerned. There is only trust.

- Conviction is our decision to stand behind our spiritual work with passionate assurance, with the belief that we are being guided to our highest and greatest good each moment of our lives. When we embody this kind of conviction we choose to follow our spiritual path with fervor, courage, fortitude, patience and love. This is how we approach all of our spiritual journeying, even our Sacred Sign work.

- Principle is the standard by which we choose to live our lives. Spiritual principle is the unshakable acceptance that we are one with the Universe and it cannot be wrong. It is the absolute acceptance that the Universe is always there to direct us, and will never misguide nor hurt us in any way. When we live by this

- Idea is the notion that belief is conceived in the mind, and is a decision or choice. Our mind is very powerful. When we conceive the idea that we should believe in the goodness and guidance of the Universe, we send a message to Spirit that is positive and life-affirming. In turn, the Universe sends us more reasons to believe in its goodness. It is the Universal Law of Return. A loving God rewards belief in his/her goodness with blessings untold.

Once you have decided to believe with every fiber of your being, you are then free to look for spiritual answers without fear of ridicule or mistake. Even though sacred signs are sometimes hard to discern, when you believe, you become patient waiting for them to unfold, without questioning them at every turn.

Step #3: Surrender

The last step is the hardest. Once you are strong in your belief/faith, you must surrender all of your doubt, fear, difficulties, problems, hurts, pains, upsets, or disappointments, to Spirit. When you surrender you tell the Universe that you no longer wish to deal with all of life's difficulties alone, and you request and accept divine assistance. You are admitting that you have ultimate trust in God/Goddess to handle the uncomfortable situations of your life for you. Again, it is our human tendency to want to affect every situation that occurs in our lives. There is nothing wrong in wanting to participate in our good, and the creation of our future. What is dangerous is our assertion that we can and should do it all ourselves. The thought that only our decisions are truly accurate, and that we really don't need help from anyone, let alone God (if He truly exists), is harmful to our spiritual well-being. There is a stubborn insistence within us that claims to have all the answers and refuses to see that there is more to life than meets the eye. When we are truly able to let go of this resistance, we will be on the road to surrender, and to a life that is rich with spiritual assistance and endless possibilities.

Here is what surrendering means:

- Surrender means you are willing to allow Spirit to guide you, without question.

- Surrender means you are willing to accept Spirit's advice beyond the shadow of a doubt.

- Surrender means that you no longer expect to control the outcome of the situation.

- Surrender means you give up the struggle of trying to manipulate your life.

- Surrender means you bet in flow with your destiny by listening to and following the divine guidance.

- Surrender means you no longer try to figure everything out before you take action.

- Surrender means you trust that God hears your prayers and requests.

- Surrender means you believe, without question, that you are always being led to your highest good.

Surrender is the ultimate climate of trust. It is an unequivocal belief that all is well in your life because you are in direct union with your Creator, the Source of the Universe. It is a mighty choice but one that will make all of your spiritual work uplifting and effortless. Sacred Signs will become messengers of truth to you that pave the way to greater understanding and problem-solving in this lifetime.

Since this issue of trust is a perplexing one, it will help to look at the entire approach to the sacred sign work process. The 9-step sacred sign process will be a helpful tool in understanding signs. It will put the information into perspective, and illustrate a practical way to synthesize the material into a workable form that will lead to spiritual success.

The 9-Step Sacred Sign Process

You are about to read what is probably the most important section of this book. It will help you to grasp the course of action of sacred sign work from start to finish in a simple 9-step formula. What follows is the ultimate synthesis of this entire system. All of the information stated prior to this has led to this point. This easily understandable format will make working with signs a simple and rewarding task. Pay close attention to these steps, write them in your journal or commit them to memory, if you like, but follow them closely:

1. Recognize that you have a need/desire/problem to be solved.

2. Decide that you wish to receive divine guidance to address your need/desire/problem.

3. Create a sacred sign statement that reflects your particular situation.

4. Perform your sacred sign ritual.

5. Make a conscious effort to look for the sign in your everyday life circumstances, people, and events.

6. Actively interpret your sign.

7. Act on the information you receive through the sign.

8. Do the inner work to stay confident and trust that Spirit guides the sign, its message, and your life, toward your highest good.

9. Observe the results of the sign's message in your life, and act accordingly to live in a state of peace and joy.

You now have the perfect formula to invoke the highest form of spiritual guidance, and the tools to make your dreams come true in your life. However, all of this is for naught if you do not trust in this process fully and undoubtedly. You must choose to trust in the Universe to support and guide you always.

A Sacred Sign Scenario

Nevertheless, if you are still having trouble understanding the absolute necessity of trust in your sacred sign work, here is a realistic scenario that might help. In it we will follow the aforementioned steps, one-by-one, and see how they unfold in a practical example.

For illustration purposes, let us say that you find yourself in deep financial distress. You have $30,000 in credit card debt. Lord knows, many of us including myself, have been there! Let us also say that you have a job that pays far less than that amount per year, and you are thinking of taking on a second job to pay off the cards. Working an additional job would mean spending less time with your family, cut down on weekend rest time, and add stress to your life. After considering these facts, you are very confused and your mind is in a tizzy, because you really don't want either situation to exist in your life. You have run the emotional and logical gamut of practical ideas in an attempt to come up with a way out of this mess, but without success. Instead of fretting, worrying, crying, thinking, wishing it wasn't so, feeling sorry for yourself, and generally placing too much energy into the negative reaction to this problem, you decide that there must be a better, more comforting, more efficient way to make this decision. Here is what to do, step-by-step:

1. Recognize that you have a need/desire/problem.

The worst thing we can do is avoid our problems. Pretending that "everything is fine" and putting on a confident face to others when our heart is breaking is just not helpful. It is much more effective to bravely and squarely look at the situation with strength and wisdom, and make a deliberate decision to stop agonizing and start seeking solutions. Therefore, you tell yourself that you have a money problem, and accept your responsibility in creating it. Admit, "I have attracted this negative energy and situation concerning money and lack, and I accept my responsibility in creating it." When you have done so, it's time to move on to the next step.

2. Decide that you wish to receive divine guidance to address the need/desire/problem.

Make a deliberate choice to include God in the solution to your dilemma. That conscious decision is powerful because it invokes all of the positive, loving energy of the Universe. Decide that your money problem needs divine assistance, and resolve to get it. We should not just turn to God when the going gets rough, but often in gratitude for what we already have. If you want to receive the gifts of the Universe, you must ask for them with a grateful heart. As illustrated in the chapter 1 affirmation, we must thank Spirit for working with us before we even get started, and we must thank our Source for giving us what we ask for in advance. This sends a message to God that we trust so wholeheartedly in his/her generosity, that we just know that we will receive the help we request. When we ask for divine guidance in this way, there is no way we will not get it! Say, "Thank you, God/Spirit, for Your divine guidance and solution to this problem."

3. Create a sacred sign statement that reflects your particular situation.

Referring back to chapter 4, let us construct a sacred sign statement for this particular situation. An extremely effective statement is, "Show me a sign that it is harmonious for me to get a second job to pay off my $30,000 credit card debt. For this I give thanks to you, God/Goddess/Spirit/Universe (pick one). And so it is!" Of course you may add timing to this request, if you wish. Now that you have formed the request, it is time to send the message.

4. Perform your sacred sign ritual.

Set up and perform your private ritual in your own sacred space. In this scenario, to receive help with money problems we have placed green stones on the altar, and a dollar bill under the candle. Performing the ritual has successfully sent your request to the Universe for a response.

5. Make a conscious effort to look for the sign in your everyday life circumstances, people, and events.

Now you are armed and ready to recognize and accept your sign. The day after you performed the Sacred Sign Ritual, you decide to bake a cake, a hobby of yours, to lighten the mood of your day—and your life, for that matter! That evening, you invite several friends over to share in the bounty, and find comfort in their presence. Over coffee, one of your friends mentions that your cakes are so delicious that you should think about selling them, as well as the other delicious goods you've created over the years. Suddenly, a light bulb goes off in your mind! You have always wanted to do that, but were never motivated. What better motivation is there than a $30,000 credit card debt? You immediately realize you might have stumbled upon a solution. But it is more than that!

6. Actively interpret your sign.

This, my friend, is your sign. Looking at it logically, what are the odds that you would receive a suggestion at this needy point in your life that suddenly makes sense? They are slim. What has transpired is divine inspiration. Your friend was divinely inspired to make that suggestion, and you were divinely inspired to consider it as a possibility now. No, it may not be profound, but it is nonetheless life-changing. See the miraculous in the mundane, and you will never misinterpret or dismiss the presence of a sacred sign again!

7. Act on the information you receive through the sign.

Divinely motivated, you begin researching how to start a home business. You find you can do this with little capital. Your friends offer their help with advertising word-of-mouth recommendations, and become your first customers. Doors fly open with each step you take to make this a reality. Before you know it, your little kitchen cake baking business supplies enough extra money to meet those credit card payments, and you are on your way to paying off those balances in full! When you are doing what you are meant to do, and following the advice of Spirit, all things flow with ease.

8. Do the inner work to stay confident and trust that Spirit guides the sign, its message, and your life, toward your highest good.

The next task you have is to remain steadfast in your belief that you are doing the right thing by following Spirit's advice, especially on those nights when you would like to be sitting in front of the TV with your feet up, but you have to bake a huge wedding cake for tomorrow's delivery. This is when your faith and trust must be renewed. Remind yourself with the affirmation, "God guides me toward my highest and greatest good each and every moment of my life. And so it is!"

9. *Observe the results of the sign's message in your life, and act accordingly to live in a state of peace and joy.*

In your moments of prayer and reflection, consider the sacred sign sent to you by a loving energy that wants to help you, and wants you to be happy. As you retrace your actions and the events that led to the current moment, you will see the sign more clearly and wonder why you hesitated at all. With each positive experience that results from each cake you sell, and each credit card bill you pay off, you will realize and accept the gift of peace and joy you have received, simply because you asked for it. What results is ultimate trust in the power that made you and loves you unconditionally.

Exercise #8

After examining the above scenario, if even one question still exists in your mind concerning trust, an exercise follows that will help you take an objective look at yourself as you learn to establish a new confidence in the Universe.

Answer the following questions and record your answers here or in the sacred sign journal. Check the appropriate response.

1. I am skeptical about spiritual or supernatural occurrences.
   Yes __ No √

2. I believe that there is a power in the Universe that loves and guides.
   Yes √ No __

3. People often look to me for advice.
   Yes √ No __

4. Generally, I have no problem giving up control, or not being in charge.
   Yes __ No √

5. I like to meditate and see the value in it.
   Yes _√_ No __

6. Trusting is easy for me.
   Yes __ No _√_

7. I am open to new ways of seeing life.
   Yes _√_ No __

8. I do not get mad easily or lose my temper quickly.
   Yes __ No _√_

9. My fears do not overwhelm me.
   Yes __ No _√_

10. I am a self-confident person.
    Yes _√_ No __

11. When things go wrong in my life, I do not worry about them.
    Yes __ No _√_

12. I seldom get depressed.
    Yes _√_ No __

13. I seek the help of others when I'm in need.
    Yes _√_ No __

14. My beliefs are strong and unshakable.
    Yes _√_ No __

15. I accept that I can have all that I desire in life.
    Yes _√_ No __

16. Others' opinions do not influence my thinking.
    Yes _√_ No __

17. I am not stubborn.
    Yes___ No ⟍

18. I pray often.
    Yes ⟍ No ___

19. I'm constantly looking for ways to improve myself and my life.
    Yes ✓ No ___

Evaluate your answers. Count the number of "yes" and "no" responses and calculate a total.

Total # of "yes" answers ___12___   Total # of "no" answers ___7___

If the total of "yes" answers is larger than the total of "no" answers, congratulations! You are considered a trusting person by spiritual standards. If your totals are about half-and-half in each category you are not a completely trusting person, and might sabotage your efforts with doubt when working with Sacred Signs. The good news is that there is hope for you, because you are not totally closed to the possibility of divine guidance entering your life. To remove any obstacles in your mind that you might not be aware of, affirm the following statement often, until you feel confident and ready:

> *I thank God/Goddess/Spirit for your sacred messages, and I release any remaining doubt or fear as I open to divine wisdom. And so it is!*

That should do the trick. However, if the total of "no" answers is larger than the total of "yes" answers you have a lot more work to do! Distrust, not just in spiritual matters, but also in all areas of life is an indicator that you are fearful, angry, opinionated, stubborn, depressed, closed-minded, and generally separated from your highest good. Ugh! It is not as bad as it sounds. With positive, dedicated effort, all these attitudes may be changed.

If you want to do sacred sign work and receive messages and guidance from the Universe, you must make an effort to change the way you perceive life. Try to see the positive instead of the negative in every situation. See difficulties as opportunities to grow and become a better, more spiritual being. Choose to think differently now! To help you do this, I suggest that at least three times a day you affirm:

I release any and all blocks, past and present, to trusting in God/Goddess/ Spirit/Universe. I am secure in the knowledge that I am divinely loved and protected. For this, I give thanks. And so it is!

The Key #3 affirmation will free you from your inner demons and open your heart to a world you never dreamed existed.

Key #3 Meditation

Trust

Find a comfortable position in your chair, hands on your lap, and feet flat on the floor. Close your eyes and take three gentle breaths, inhale through the nose, and exhale through the mouth. . . . Continue breathing gently with mouth closed. As you do, feel a wave of relaxation moving from the top of your head, slowly down, down, down, to the tips of your toes. . . . Breathe gently and allow yourself to feel what it would be like to trust completely that all your needs will be met in this life, and all your problems will reach solutions that are right and perfect for you. . . . Relax for a few moments as you contemplate these feelings. . . . Experience relief, comfort, joy, as you release struggle, strain, doubt, fear, and anger. As you relax within this experience, remain completely at peace, and invite God/Goddess/Spirit/Universe to be a part of your life. Silently say that you are grateful for whatever messages you might receive, and that you trust in God's ultimate wisdom to guide you to your highest good. . . . As you continue to breathe gently, inhale peace and tranquility, and exhale all tension. Be calm in the knowledge that your words have been heard, and vow to never withhold your love and trust from Spirit. . . . After a few moments, and when you are ready, take another gentle breath, and as you exhale, return to full consciousness and open your eyes.

Key #3 Affirmation

Trust

Thank you, God/Goddess/Spirit/Universe for my ultimate trust in your wisdom. I have unlimited faith in your guidance, and I am certain that you always act in my highest and greatest good. I am strong, confident, safe, and happy, as I turn over my problems, difficulties, and struggles to you. In return, I receive peace, understanding, and insight beyond my imaginings. And so it is!"

Important Points to Remember

- Trust, believe, and surrender.

- When you truly trust in and believe that you have received a Sacred Sign, all doubt vanishes and relief replaces fear.

- If you send energy of distrust, you get back more reasons to be distrustful.

- Logic may be your worst enemy in interpreting and believing in Sacred Signs.

- Do not question a sign with logic when it appears.

- Try not to let doubt defeat the sign work over time.

- Stay trustful even if you do not receive the answer you were hoping for.

- When interpreting signs, actively make parallels in your mind as they apply to your life.

- Use affirmations to remove doubt and fear.

- Make a vow to believe in a greater power than your ego.

- Forget the past and trust yourself.

- Do not doubt your inner voice.

- Resist putting yourself down.

- Expect the best.

- Don't be afraid to think differently.

- Allow yourself to be vulnerable.

- Believe that with God all things are possible.

- Belief is God in action within our lives in the form of faith, conviction, principle, and idea.

- Surrender means many things, but most importantly that you have trust that the Universe will lovingly remove all obstacles from your life.

- Follow the 9-step sacred sign process diligently.

Working with Your Divine Destiny

Chapter Seven

What to Do When Your Sign Appears

Sacred signs are divine destiny in action. They are the direct manifestation of our communication with God. Signs are important because they are answers to our prayers. That is what makes them sacred. When you receive a sign you have received a direct response from God. Everyone is privy to this wonderful gift, and when you begin to get these responses your life becomes easier and easier, and what's more, you really feel in touch with your divine Source. You will also recognize your inner power. That is most remarkable because most of us see ourselves and our existence on this Earth as ordinary and uneventful. What greater event is there than a "hello" from God? This is what keeps us spiritual seekers on track. A steady supply of heavenly knowledge will do that for you! But if you are new to sign work you might be asking, "What do I do when my sign manifests into my life?" It just so happens, I can help you with that.

We usually experience two responses to a sign's appearance in our lives. Our reaction might be positive or it might be negative. They both evoke certain emotional responses. Some of the positive emotions we might feel are joy, relief, clarity, assurance of the existence of God, pleasure, certainty, or resolve. But then there are the negative responses such as panic, disbelief, denial, indecision, doubt, or fear. Even those who believe that they are ready for their sign or who have done this work before, might experience either positive or negative reactions depending upon the importance of the situation. If you are asking for a sign to clarify whether you should purchase a particular sofa, and the sign appears to give you a "no" answer, your reaction might not be as intense as if you were asking for clarity concerning a career or dramatic lifestyle change. It is obviously all relative. We don't always like the answer we receive, but we must be ready for it, or there is really no point in asking in the first place.

Sign Appearance Checklist

I assume that if you are reading this book, you are willing to believe in and follow your signs. Yet, there might still be some confusion when you are new at this sort of spiritual work. You might not be clear as to how to proceed from this point, or how to integrate the message the sign has delivered into your life. If this is true for you, I have outlined a simple procedure to follow, as a kind of checklist, to help you. Here is what you should do when your sign appears:

1. Check that you perceived your sign correctly, and say a prayer of thanks.

2. Make sure that you interpreted the message of the sign correctly.

3. Record the results in the sacred sign journal for further understanding and future reference.

4. Follow the advice the sign recommends.

5. After following the advice and taking action on the message, wait for results.

6. When you have recognized results, say a prayer of thanks.

7. Now you may move on to ask for other signs.

Let us review each step in detail.

1. Check that you perceived your sign correctly, and say a prayer of thanks.

Refer back to previous chapters in which you formulated your Sacred Sign State-ment. Refresh your memory as to what you have requested and the reason for ask-ing. If you have asked for a specific sign, there should be no problem when it ap-pears. If you have left the design of your sign up to the Universe, have remained aware and ready for it, then you should perceive it correctly. To assure that you have perceived the sign correctly, put the pieces of your synchronistic events together in your mind, and review the process through which your sign manifested. Once you are certain your sign has manifested, say a prayer of thanks. Remember, gratitude is a magnet for good, when it is expressed sincerely.

2. Make sure that you interpreted the message of the sign correctly.

The message is more important that the sign itself. Review the chapters to un-derstand whether you received a "yes" or "no" answer. If you have constructed your request statement well, interpreting your message should be easy.

3. Record the results in the sacred sign journal for further understand-ing and future reference.

It is very important to record your results, especially if you are new at this work. It is also necessary if you wish to observe a pattern in your sign work. Years later, I have referred back to my sacred sign journal, and found very helpful information concerning my own spiritual growth over the years. You will find that you are not simply recording results. You are chronicling your life experiences.

4. Follow the advice the sign indicates.

Of course, it is your free will choice to either follow the advice of the sign or not.

I highly recommend that you do. If you ignore the advice, you will send a message to Spirit that you do not trust in divine help, and you will receive many more reasons to be distrustful. The Universal Law of Reciprocity is powerful. Therefore, when you realize and understand the answer, act on it. I cannot say this more emphatically. You will not regret it.

5. After following the advice and taking action on the message, wait for results.

Patience is the operative word here. When you act upon the message you need to tell yourself that you are prepared to wait for the final results of your actions. Sit back and relax. Remember that you asked Spirit to give you a sign, and an answer to your request that would be in your highest good. How can anything else result?

6. When you have recognized results, say a prayer of thanks.

As always, as soon as you realize that you have received your sign, immediately say a prayer of thanks. Do the same when you have perceived closure after acting upon the sign. Gratitude is very important. It tells God that you are trusting in divine counsel, and are open and ready to receive it with a willing heart.

7. Now you may move on to ask for other signs.

At this point, you are ready to ask for a different sign for another situation with which you need assistance. You should not ask for more than one Sacred Sign at a time so that you do not scatter your energy, and confuse the situation for yourself. *Move on to asking for a new sign only when you have recognized, interpreted, and acted upon the previous one.*

After reviewing the checklist, if there is still doubt in your mind as to the validity of signs, take a look at the following steps for further clarification. You didn't think I'd leave you with a shred of anxiety, did you? Read and rejoice!

For Further Clarification

If you are still not sure that you:

A. got your sign,

B. understand your sign, or

C. know what to do to follow your sign's advice,

then:

1. Check that you have followed the steps and asked for your original sign correctly.

2. Ask for a clarification sign.

3. If you do not believe you received a clarification sign, then ask for your original sign again and do the following:

1. Reword your sacred sign statement.

    A. Eliminate the time element.

    B. Omit a specific sign request.

2. Repeat the affirmations that remove doubt and blocks.

3. Remain aware, and look for the sign each day.

4. Put all doubt and anxiety out of your mind by saying the affirmations that build trust, belief, and openness.

5. Continue to be patient, and wait peacefully.

All of these safeguards should work for you. I have developed them over the years and they have never let me down! Most of all, stay calm, have faith, and know that you can always try again.

When Unexpected Signs Appear

There is a circumstance that might occur in your life when you least expect it—the appearance of a sign you did not request. Yes, the Universe is miraculous and can actually read your mind. Sometimes when we are wrestling with a situation or problem in our lives, God just steps in and lets us know what to do (or what not to do) in a spontaneous fashion. These signs manifest through a series of related negative or positive events. I have talked about the signs that arrive unannounced in an earlier chapter, but what do you do when you think you're getting a message through synchronistic events? You respond in the same way you would, had you requested the sign yourself.

I often receive unexpected signs, as will you, because I am open to receiving the messages and assistance from Spirit. Each day I let the Universe know in my prayers that I am open, willing, and ready to receive the best it has to offer. This positive energy attracts divine advice in any number of ways. One of those ways is through the random appearance of sacred signs in my life. As I write this book, I continue to experience them quite often.

Several weeks ago, I received a telephone call from my health insurance company informing me that my benefit year would be up in two months, and that I must make any changes to my plan at that time. It was a courtesy call I received every year and thought little of it. Several days later I received a bill from my doctor's office for treatments dated several years past. I thought that these procedures were covered by my insurance. Upon a visit to the doctor's office, I was told that those procedures were not covered, and much to my dismay, I was expected to pay hundreds of dollars, on the spot, for services done three years ago. Needless to say, I was outraged because my monthly insurance payment was nearly $400, with a $1000 deductible, and now I was expected to pay for services I was previously told were covered. When I spoke with the insurance company they said I was, in fact, responsible. I filed this event away in my consciousness and resolved to pay the bill.

The next day, I received another statement of financial responsibility for $150 for an office visit from one year ago. To top it all off, that same week I received a notification letter from my insurance company that my rate would be increasing in several months! It was clearly a sign. This was too much. The monthly payment was already very high, and since I am self-employed, it took a large chunk out of my monthly income. I began to assess the synchronistic events of the past two weeks, and realized that I was getting a strong sign from the Universe concerning my insurance.

This series of events motivated me to take action. I decided to look for another company and a better deal. I knew I was being told by Spirit to do something about my insurance situation, and being a serious sign worker, I dutifully set out to heed the message of my spontaneous sacred sign.

The previous year, I attempted to find another insurance company because of the rising cost of my current insurance, but to no avail. Other companies offered even higher rates to self-employed individuals, so I decided to stick with my original program. Then something amazing happened.

During the weeks of this strange series of events, I heard a radio commercial that offered a reduced rate of health insurance to self-employed folks through the State of New York. I immediately began inquiring about it, found a company that administered it, applied, and was accepted, all within a week, and well in advance of the end of my benefit year with the original company. The most astounding part of this story is that my monthly payment was lowered from $400 to $160 dollars per month! Divine intervention responded to my subconscious desire. Isn't that something? Pay attention to related events that seem to be leading you toward a more harmonious and abundant life.

If that example is not enough to convince you to heed your spontaneous signs, and act upon them, here is another.

Years ago, I was in a relationship that ended badly. I was heartbroken because I cared for my partner very much. After the breakup, I just went on with my life as we all do in such circumstances.

As time went on, I had a string of discouraging dates, but nothing worked out as a long-term possibility. I began wondering if I should attempt reconciliation with my former boyfriend, even though I hadn't seen him for many years. Then the signs started to come, unannounced.

One evening I was out with a girlfriend, and I was lamenting the lack of quality men out there in "dating land." Out of the blue, she suggested that I contact my former boyfriend, and propose reconciliation. Imagine my shock when her words seemed to echo my recent thoughts. Still, I did nothing.

About one week later, I had a surprise visitor to my office. It was a former client, whom I hadn't seen in about two years. It just so happened that she had been a very close friend of my ex-boyfriend. She knew him very well. I was stunned to see her, realizing the spiritual connection to my recent conversation with my friend. My visitor said she was just driving by my office building, and felt the need to stop in to say hello. Our conversation lasted two hours, during which she assured me that ending the relationship was for the best. I was immensely relieved, and the grief and guilt ended right then and there, as well as any thoughts of reconciliation.

I know Spirit sent her to me that day. She was my sacred sign. The Universe further convinced me the next week when I stumbled upon a television show specifically describing the symptoms of "commitment-phobic men." My former boyfriend fit the profile to a "T".

When I had sufficiently digested and synthesized this unexpected information from the Universe, I realized that I was being advised not to take the specific action I had entertained concerning reconciliation with my former partner. The synchronistic events seemed to reassure me that I had made the right decisions for myself in the past. I decided that the sacred message was not to pursue a future with him again, and to let the relationship go forever. I cannot describe the sense of peace I experienced. This sign was a true gift from Spirit, for which I am most grateful.

So, you see, you, too may experience such gifts if you are aware. With unexpected signs, as with all other sacred signs, you must heed the message and follow the advice. It will always result in your highest and greatest good.

Exercise #9

This is a short exercise designed to help you know if you have been clear about your desires, executed your sign work well, and have created the best possible environment for success.

Answer the following questions checking a simple "Yes" or "No" response. For best results, think about them for a while, even though they seem simple at first.

1. I am very sure that I know what I want the sacred sign to indicate.
   Yes __ No __

2. I am willing to do all it takes to interpret the sign's message.
   Yes __ No__

3. I have constructed a sacred sign statement that embodies the full intention of my needs.
Yes __ No __

4. I have affirmed to remove all doubt concerning this work.
Yes __ No __

5. I have resolved to be fully aware and look for my sign in my daily life.
Yes __ No __

6. I will have no trouble keeping my work to myself, and not sharing my process with others.
Yes __ No __

7. I trust in the Universe to hear and answer my request beyond the shadow of a doubt.
Yes __ No __

8. I am prepared to wait patiently for my sign to enter my life.
Yes __ No __

9. I will recognize spontaneous signs when they appear, and treat their messages just as I would requested signs.
Yes __ No __

10. I will always express gratitude to God/Goddess/Spirit/Universe for all that I have, and all that is yet to be.
Yes __ No __

If you answered "yes" to each question, you are absolutely ready to reap the unlimited benefits the Universe has to offer. If you had even one "no" answer, you are definitely not ready for sacred sign work. I recommend that you go back to the affirmations and release your blocks. You will intuitively know when you have done so. Then you may proceed with your dialogue with the Universe.

Sign Appearance Meditation

Find a comfortable position in your chair, hands on your lap, and feet flat on the floor. Close your eyes and take three gentle breaths, inhale through the nose, and exhale through the mouth. . . . Continue breathing gently with mouth closed. As you do, feel a wave of relaxation moving from the top of your head, slowly down, down, down, to the tip of your toes. . . . Breathe gently and begin to form a mental picture of your sign. If you have asked for a specific object, see yourself receiving it. If you have left the sign up to the Universe, just relax for a few moments, and open to impressions from Spirit. Allow those impressions to form pictures in your mind. . . . See yourself at the precise instant you receive your sign. Open to its guidance. Feel how wonderful that revelation is. . . . Experience how joyful you are to finally get help with this situation. . . . Relax for a few moments as you contemplate these feelings. . . . Remain completely at peace. Now, silently thank the Divine for your sign and its guidance. Continue to breathe gently, inhale peace and tranquility and exhale all tension. . . . After a few moments, and when you are ready, take another gentle breath, and as you exhale, return to full consciousness and open your eyes.

Sign Appearance Affirmation

Thank you, God/Goddess/Spirit/Universe, for my ability to know exactly what to do when my sacred sign appears in my life. I fully trust in your divine messages, and I am willing to do what it takes to use your advice wisely. For this miraculous gift, I give thanks to you. And so it is!

Important Points to Remember

- Sacred Signs are divine destiny in action, and the direct manifestation of communication with God.

- Our reaction to the appearance of sacred signs in our lives might be either positive or negative.

- Use the sign appearance checklist to relieve confusion when doing sign work.

- Ask for a new sign only when you have recognized, interpreted, and acted upon the previous one.

- If you are still unsure that you received a sign or know what to do if you have, follow the steps under "For Further Clarification."

- Sometimes unexpected or unsolicited signs will appear in your life.

- Treat unexpected signs as you would those you requested.

- Always express gratitude to God/Goddess/Spirit/Universe for all that you have, and all that is yet to be.

Chapter Eight

Communicating Regularly with the Universe

Many people believe that it is impossible to communicate directly with the Universe. Every day, skeptics attempt to discourage those of us who choose to believe differently. Yet, I have experienced that it is not only possible to commune with heavenly energies, it is a very natural process, and one that is readily available to all human beings.

So far, you have been working with sacred signs to convey an initial message to Spirit stating that you require guidance. At first it seems like a one-way conversation, but once your sign manifests into your world, the dialogue begins. The fascinating part of this exchange is that it is actual proof that God/Goddess/Spirit/Universe is communicating with you. In silent worship moments you might not have an indication that your prayer has been heard because there is no immediate response. With signs, there is a definite, unmistakable answer transmitted to you through the energy within your world, conveyed by the Source that made you. You can never break this bond. You may cease to engage in such dialogue, which is, of course, your free will choice, but the Universe is always there, ready to resume the conversation.

The Process of Divine Communication

For ten years, I was a professor of communication arts and sciences at several distinguished universities and colleges. In teaching communication skills to hundreds of students, I used a simple model to help explain the connection. I taught that a communication occurs only when there are certain components interacting together. Here is what the model looks like:

For communication to begin there must be a *sender*, or originator, a *receiver*, or recipient, and a *message* for them to transmit. Yet, communication in its purest form does not occur unless one very vital component exists—*feedback*. Take a look:

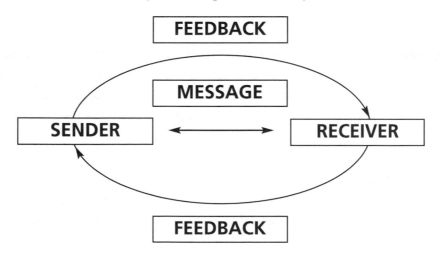

Communication in its purest form takes place only when feedback exists. Otherwise, a message sent is just that—a message sent. There is no proof, indication, or verification of that message ever arriving at its destination, and therefore, its existence as communication is questionable. Feedback is the key to the process. It is the proof that our message was successfully transmitted and received by the designated receiver. In sign work, the receivers are both God and us. In sacred sign work, feedback is obvious, and active in the equation. Therefore, one may conclude that based upon this criteria, communication must exist between us and our Creator, because after having sent our message to the Universe, we receive feedback.

Operating under this communication principle, when we request a sign we act as the sender, the Universe is the receiver, the request or sacred sign statement is the message, and the sacred sign itself is the feedback. Cool, huh? Very cool. We can never *not* communicate. As long as we live and breathe we will have some response to a message, whether it is verbal, like, "Oh my God, I got my sign!" or nonverbal, such as a thought or realization, or the sound of a gasp escaping your throat when you realize that your sign has manifested. That action is feedback. The Universe computes it as such and sends you more of what you asked for. The chain is never broken until you break it. In other words, once you receive your sign, you say "Thank you" and originate another transmission in the form of a new sign request. That way you keep the lines of communication with the Universe open.

Now you can see, through analyzing the communication model, communication with the Source of life does exist as a constant in the Universe.

God/Goddess/Spirit wants us to be happy and to have what we want in life. Don't be afraid to ask for what you want. You can never ask too much of a loving Creator. Spirit exists to expand and create through you. Pray, affirm, meditate, do your sacred sign work, and you will keep up a constant dialogue with God. We are all worthy of such special communication and should engage in it regularly.

How to Have a Conversation with God

In order to keep the dialogue flowing freely between you and Spirit, there are several steps you may take to facilitate the process. As with all our work, they are easy and only require your commitment to succeed. I have simplified the practice and narrowed it down to the ten following guidelines. They are listed and then explained in detail:

1. Be in a constant state of gratitude, and say so.

2. Perform a personal ritual each day, including prayer, affirmation, and meditation.

3. Have a series of chats with God each day, as though he/she were right there in the room with you.

4. Ask for help with whatever decisions you wish, from the mundane to the profound.

5. Make every effort to remain in a spiritual mind-frame, with an unshakable belief in your connection to the Divine.

6. Talk with your heavenly teachers/guides/angels/loved ones often, as you do your Source.

7. Turn over all of your problems to Spirit. Talk them over with the Universe and wait for divine solutions without concern.

8. Every evening, review the moments of divine communication you experienced during the day.

9. Share with and teach others the spiritual tools you have discovered, and ask the Universe how you may best do that.

10. Continue to send only positive, loving energy into the world.

Now let's get specific!

1. Be in a constant state of gratitude, and say so.

Tell the Universe that you appreciate all that it has given you every chance you get. Not only will this get you more of what you want, it will uplift and comfort you. My students and clients tell me that when they get into a rhythm of working with the Universe, they find themselves expressing their gratitude all the time. They say that they realize just how blessed they are once they begin *to pay attention* to all they are receiving. Your gratitude statements may be just as simple and personal as you want them to be. You need not have a model for this, but I usually say, "Thanks, God, for this, for all that I have, and for all that is yet to be. And so it is!" God will get the message even if you just say a simple, "Thanks." Be sure to do it often! Your blessings will be immeasurable.

2. Perform a personal ritual each day, including prayer, affirmation, and meditation.

To continue the dialogue with Spirit, one must make a commitment to it each day. Yes, I know that, in today's world, commitment is a scary word. But, when you make a commitment to God you open up a world of unlimited possibilities. Once you get used to your daily practice, it will become as comfortable as washing your face each morning.

It will not take long to open to the Universe. My suggestion is that you do so when you first get up in the morning, before you set out on your chores, and possibly, even before getting out of bed. I have found that time of day to be most effective, because there is less distraction while you are still in bed. If you live with others, you may do your ritual before they rise, as well. The quiet of the early morning or late evening is peaceful and calming.

Each morning, before rising out of bed, I do a ritual that includes prayer, affirmation, and meditation. They are the three magical components. Specifically, I sit up in bed, and do the following:

- Take three cleansing breaths, inhaling through the nose, and exhaling through the mouth. You may do this with eyes open or shut.

- After breathing, I say the following prayer:

Good morning, God. Thank you for this day, and for _____
(insert your special thanks, such as gratitude for family, friends, your job, your home, etc.), I welcome you into my life, and thank you for helping me do your work in the world today, whatever form it may take. Guide me, teach me, and lead me to my highest and greatest good. And so it is!

- Universe to send me some feedback, in the form of inner peace. Sometimes a specific message will come through as a visualization or intuitive knowing, which helps me get through my day in a positive way. When I feel I have complete peace, I take another gentle breath, and open my eyes.

- The last step in my personal ritual is an affirmation. I positively state the following, beyond the shadow of a doubt:

I am open to the best the Universe has to offer me, today. I receive it, accept it, and so it is!

That is it. It is a simple and very effective way to start your day, while keeping those lines of communication open to the Universe. The ritual will only take a few moments, five at the most. Extending that time is up to you. As you work with your personal ritual, you will develop your own comfortable prayers and affirmations. Give it time, and don't give up! Soon, you will hear a word from God every day!

3. Have a series of chats with God each day, as though he/she were right there in the room with you.

I have found that my relationship with our Creator has become more and more real for me because I consider God to be my constant companion. I do not go around introducing him/her to all the folks I meet, but I do recognize that energy in a personal way. Specifically, I chat with Spirit constantly, throughout my day, as though my best friend was right in the room with me, and we were sharing an intimate conversation. I tell God my thoughts. Although I know that Spirit already knows my thoughts, it helps me to voice them. I make comments all day to God as my life unfolds. I say things like, "Thanks, God. I appreciate that those new shoes I want are on sale today!" or, "Give me the strength to get through this one!" when a difficult confrontation arises with another person. There really isn't anything that I do not chat about. I even ask God's opinion on things. I might say, "Okay, God. Should I go straight home after work, or run those errands I've been postponing?" I always get feedback, because I pay attention to what is happening in my world. My feedback comes in many ways, but mostly in an intuitive sense of knowing just what to do, or not to do. God lets me know if I should go straight home today or run errands through a *silent, intense feeling* I get to do one thing or the other. Then as I proceed to do what I am sensing is right at that moment, a sense of peace and calm comes over me. When I ignore or disregard that feeling, I tend to experience anxiety on some level, like impatience, or doubt. I have learned to listen to the voice of Spirit within me, and follow it. You will know how to recognize God communicating with you with practice and attention. I am sure many of you already do!

4. Ask for help with whatever decisions you wish, from the mundane to the profound.

Remember that your buddy, God, is a very personal energy, albeit a very profound one as well. Still, as your Creator and friend, Spirit will guide you at every turn if you just ask. Feel free to ask for anything, from, "Where should I park at the Galleria Mall?" to, "Should I ask Shirley to marry me?" Believe me, the Universe wants to help you with all of it. Keeping open to communication with this divine energy will help you through every major decision of your life. The benefits greatly outweigh the efforts you have to make to keep in touch. Try it. You will see for yourself. These benefits extend far beyond your Sacred Sign work. When you get used to asking for anything and everything and you start to receive responses, your life automatically becomes richer, more abundant, and joyful, just because you now have your spiritual mentor with you at all times. You will never feel alone again.

5. Make every effort to remain in a spiritual mind-frame, with an unshakable belief in your connection to the Divine.

Communicating with the Divine on a steady basis requires us to be convinced that we can and are doing it. Questioning this connection will weaken it. It is that simple. When we live our lives with the deep spiritual conviction that we are loved and cared for by a benevolent and generous Universe, we transmit that love to others and keep the connection going forever. As human beings, we must remind ourselves often of the connection we have to our spiritual selves. It is from this steady mind`set that we grow in confidence, trust, and acceptance of our ability to transcend difficulties, and live the life of our dreams. Believe that you have a divine connection, and you will. Communicate with God through sacred sign work, through prayer, affirmation, and ritual, and in daily conversation, and that connection strengthens and expands. Consequently, you live a wondrous, marvelous existence.

6. Talk with your heavenly teachers/guides/angels/loved ones often, as you do your Source.

Spirit has set up this wonderful network of divine helpers to assist us in living out these lives we have chosen. These helpers appear in our lives as teachers, guides, angels, and loved ones who have passed on. They work with us from the spirit realm to help us focus our energies on our highest and greatest good. We each have an angel and a spirit guide appointed by God to be with us through this lifetime. I am sure many of you reading this book are well aware of these entities. If you are not, see the glossary of this book for a brief explanation, and the bibliography for further study. Your loved ones who have passed away are also available to help you, as are those who are spiritual master teachers such as Jesus Christ, Buddha, Krishna, et al. Teachers of every human need are also available to us. Just call upon them. When you do your sign work, ask your guides and angels to help you recognize the sign, and add their energies to assist you in understanding and interpreting them. The point is to ask often. Even if you do not know who these helpers are specifically, just trust in the fact that they are with you, and call upon them for help when you need it.

7. Turn over all of your problems to Spirit. Talk them over with the Universe and wait for divine solutions without concern.

This step is a simple one. Surrender is a concept we have talked about earlier in this book. When you turn over your problems to God, you get help faster than if you try to control everything yourself. This dialogue is necessary to keeping the communication flowing through all the types of spiritual work you do, which includes sign work. Ask for your signs, and trust that they will be arriving shortly. Verbally tell the Universe, "I do not really know what to do with this problem or how to solve it myself, so I am turning it over to you for a divine solution. Thanks for the help." Then wait. Be patient, and observe your life. The feedback is forthcoming. Trust that and do not ever doubt your deservedness or Spirit's love for you.

8. Every evening, review the moments of divine communication you experienced during the day.

At night, I enjoy looking back at my day. Something wonderful happens to me every day. I do have difficulties, just like anyone else, but they are always balanced by a loving occurrence. Sometimes someone will be difficult or unkind to me on a specific day, or my car will need work, or I am running late. These are stresses that we all experience. Yet, on that same day, something lovely will happen that offsets it. For example, someone will stop by my office with some kind and loving words to express, a letter arrives in the mail with a donation for my church, or I receive a phone call from someone I love, but haven't seen in a while. These events redeem the day, so to speak, and validate that there is a loving energy in the Universe reassuring me that all is well. I review all of these blessings and difficulties at the end of my day, give thanks for them, and ask God to continue to communicate with me through these moments, so that I may experience all that I need, to grow in light, love, and peace. Each night I pray:

Thank you, God, for this day, and everyone and everything in it. And so it is!

9. Share with and teach others the spiritual tools you have discovered, and ask the Universe how you may best do that.

When you truly feel you have mastered your sacred sign work, or any other spiritual tool, concept, or belief, share it with others. This is a sure-fire way to stay in communication with God. Spirit is aware of your sharing and blesses it. Each time you give of your gifts without expectation of return, you draw God closer to you. This is very handy in the communication process, because as you live a life of gratitude and giving, your dialogue with the Source gets easier and easier. If you are unsure of how you may make your contribution to the world, just ask how you may serve. You will get the answer!

10. Continue to send only positive, loving energy into the world.

It is far easier to be negative in this world than it is to be positive. Positive thoughts take work. So much seems wrong with the world that we can easily get caught up in negative thinking, to the point where our words tend to be more critical, doubtful, and hopeless. When you find yourself influenced by unexpected disappointments, or feel the tendency to make a judgment about someone, or the world in general, just stop that thought. Stop right in mid-sentence if you must, but do not allow such negativity to be a part of your reality. If you do, that is what you will attract. That dialogue you worked so hard to establish with Spirit will be curtailed, and possibly halted with each and every negative thought you express. It will affect your success with sign work, as well. To keep God alive, joy in your heart, and steady communication with the Divine, keep negativity at bay by thinking and expressing positive, loving energy in all you say and do.

Exercise #10

You now have the tools necessary to keep that communication with the Universe up and running regularly. If you follow these principles, you will have a lifetime of constant communication with the most powerful source of love, joy, abundance, and perfection that exists. But just in case there still remains any doubt, here is the final exercise, designed to help you stay open to the messages from the Universe, however they may appear in your life.

Finish these sentences as honestly as you can. Remember, they are for your eyes only. Be frank about your feelings. It is necessary to purge any remaining doubts or fears when working with Spirit, so take this opportunity to fine-tune your life, and begin reaping the rewards of your labors. Record the answers here or in the sacred sign journal.

1. In the past, I have been afraid of communicating or working with the Universe because

_____

_____

_____

_____

2. I have always felt that asking for signs or communicating with the Universe was

_____

_____

_____

_____

3. I am afraid that I might not be able to

_____

_____

_____

_____

4. All it would take for me to be a true believer in sacred sign work and communication with Spirit is

_____

_____

_____

_____

Looking back over your answers, observe the patterns within your past belief system. Only you can make this analysis. Honestly evaluate your feelings. Release those that seem to be limiting, and change them into positive, unlimited thoughts. Now complete the following statement as your grand finale and permanent good-bye to doubt and fear!

I am a true believer in working with Spirit on all levels of communication because

_____

_____

_____

Communication Meditation

Find a comfortable position in your chair, hands on your lap, and feet flat on the floor. Close your eyes and take three gentle breaths, inhale through the nose, and exhale through the mouth. . . . Continue breathing gently with mouth closed. As you do, feel a wave of relaxation moving from the top of your head, slowly down, down, down, to the tip of your toes. . . . Breathe gently and tell yourself that you are now ready and open to begin a life-long dialogue with the Universe. Feel how wonderful that connection is. . . . Experience how joyful you are to finally break through your doubts and become a friend to your Creator. . . . Vow that you will always resist constricting, limiting thoughts, and remain in constant communication with your Divine mentor. Relax for a few moments as you contemplate these feelings. . . . Remain completely at peace. Now, silently thank the Spirit for this realization. Continue to breathe gently, inhale peace and tranquility, and exhale all tension. . . . After a few moments, and when you are ready, take another gentle breath, and as you exhale, return to full consciousness and open your eyes.

Communication Affirmation

Thank you, God/Goddess/Spirit/Universe, for giving me this wonderful opportunity to communicate with you. I promise to always remain open to your divine advice, and I am ready to receive your influence each day of my life. And so it is!

Important Points to Remember

- It is possible to communicate with God on a daily basis.

- Communicating with the Divine is a natural process for all human beings.

- For communication to begin with the Universe there must be a *sender, receiver* and *message* to transmit.

- Communication in its purest form does not exist unless there is feedback.

- In sacred sign work, you are the *sender*, the Universe is the *receiver*, and your intention, request, or sacred sign statement is the *message*. The sacred sign is the *feedback*.

- We may have a conversation with God by following ten important guidelines.

- Tell the Universe that you appreciate all that it has given you, every chance you get.

- To continue the dialogue with Spirit, one must make a commitment to it each day.

- Develop a personal relationship with the Universe by having a "chat" each day.

- Spirit wants to guide you through all your decisions in life, from the simple to the profound.

- Questioning your connection to God will weaken it. Believe without doubt.

- Talk often with your angels, spirit guides, master teachers, and loved ones in spirit, as you do your Source, and ask for their assistance.

- Turn over your problems to God.

- Share what you have learned with others.

- Transform negative thoughts into positive ones and send that loving energy into the world.

Chapter Nine

Living Your Highest and Greatest Good

This is a very different chapter. It connects sacred sign work to the concept of how we may live the very best life we can. Throughout this book you have learned that if you have a sincere need, the Universe is more than willing to help you fill that need, and that sacred signs are one way of relaying that need to God. You have understood that you may communicate with Spirit, your Source, your Creator, at any given moment. In previous chapters, you have been given instruction on how to construct effective requests of the Universe in the form of sacred sign statements, learned the three mistake-proof keys to working with the Universe, and mastered the tools necessary for success. But in this chapter, you will learn an even more valuable lesson that goes beyond your connection to God.

It does seem strange that I would suggest that there is something greater in the Universe than our connection to God. What is greater is the need to make that connection a living, working, vital force in your life, and in the world. To live our highest good means that we live the life of our dreams, and help others to do so, as well. It implies that we intuitively know what is right for us, and we voluntarily follow that guidance in all we do. Our greatest good comes to us when we accept that it is possible to live a happy and fulfilling life, and not a moment sooner. It becomes our reality when we transcend the challenges life presents to us with a loving and patient heart. We recognize our very human nature, forgive it, and learn to let negativity and grief be just brief moments in our consciousness. Then we help others to do the same.

Until we learn to live and breathe our beliefs, without imposing them upon others, we are simply a mouthpiece for change but not a catalyst for it. Therefore, I am dedicating this chapter to all of us who need to make the leap from learning to doing. What you have learned here needs to be practiced in your daily life.

Living our highest and greatest good is a lot easier than one might believe. Spirit wants this for us, and nothing less. Yes, it does sound profound, but while it is a lofty concept, it is also a doable one. It is meant to be. Why would a loving Creator set a goal that his creation could not ever attain? That would not be loving, would it? Therefore, God gives us the means, sacred sign work, for one, to attain this goal of blissful living. What Spirit does not do, however, is force us to use it. That is up to our free will. *We must choose to live our highest and greatest good.* Once we choose joy, we see our way clearly to our highest good, because no negativity gets in the way. Our thoughts become positive and productive, we no longer judge others, and we look forward to each day with a renewed sense of happiness and wonder. All it takes is choice.

Along with sacred sign work and other spiritual skills, I have found it most rewarding to live my life practicing positive spiritual psychology. Viewing our lives as constantly blessed, seeing the positive side to a negative situation, and turning to our Creator for solace, guidance, problem solving, and companionship, is the way to achieve eternal bliss in an other than blissful world. The blessed combination that includes dedication to living a sacred life, commitment to personal spiritual growth, and determination to serve God and all life on the Earth is the ultimate formula for a joyful, fulfilling, abundant, prosperous, and peaceful life.

With this in mind, I have created a list of what I believe are helpful guidelines. These twenty-two guidelines were formed from my fifteen years of experience following my own spiritual path, studying, teaching, and counseling others, and all of the sacred choices and events of my life, which have led me to this moment. This list is by no means complete, but rather, it is a work in progress, constantly growing as we grow. It is changing and expanding with each loving thought we have.

Your Final Exercise

There is no formal exercise included in this chapter except this. I simply ask that of the following twenty-two statements, you note the ones that seem to jump out at you and make you say, "Hmmm." Highlight them, and record them in your Sacred Sign Journal. Meditate on them, and work with them. They are very important because they are the lessons you have yet to master. Your response to them is your higher consciousness at work, balancing and harmonizing your life. Accept this challenge and forge ahead like the brave spiritual seeker you are! Now take heart, and plunge into the list. I leave you with this expression of my true God-Selfhood, to yours.

How to Receive Your Highest and Greatest Good

1. Give thanks to our Creator for all that you have, and all that is yet to be.

2. Release fear and face life with eager anticipation of your highest good.

3. Welcome your ignorance, your "not knowing," as a gift.

4. Use logic as a tool, not as the only path to problem solving or decision-making.

5. Remember that you are a spiritual being living a human life.

6. Enter into the gap regularly—meditate each day.

7. Affirm your highest good—speak well of yourself and others.

8. Accept your faults and the faults of others without judgment—practice forgiveness.

9. Be the most loving person you can be.

10. Cultivate compassion for people, animals, and the Earth.

11. Be a good steward of all you receive—money, talent, love, material possessions.

12. Do not let others lead you where your heart does not want to go.

13. Rely on God/Goddess/Spirit to guide you through difficult times.

14. Blame no one.

15. Move forward into the world with a sense of joy and zest for life.

16. Give others your time, money, help, without expectation.

17. Always expect that you will have help from God with all your needs, and that you are never alone.

18. Give others the best of who you are, and they will return the same to you.

19. Always try to see the entire picture of a situation, rather than only that which serves your ego.

20. Value others as you do yourself, and their needs as equal to your own.

21. Give to others all that you wish for yourself.

22. Be the walking example of God on Earth.

If you set out to master these guidelines, you have made a commitment to honor your Source, yourself, and the world. With this focus your life will begin to manifest joy, wealth, health, and love beyond your greatest expectation. Your highest and greatest good and that of all who are in your life will blossom and grow. If you don't believe me, just ask for a sign!

I wish you light, love, and peace.

Highest and Greatest Good Meditation

Find a comfortable position in your chair, hands on your lap, and feet flat on the floor. Close your eyes and take three gentle breaths, inhale through the nose, and exhale through the mouth. . . . Continue breathing gently with mouth closed. As you do, feel a wave of relaxation moving from the top of your head, slowly down, down, down, to the tips of your toes. . . . Breathe gently and visualize yourself living your perfect life. See the home in which you live, your loved ones by your side, your perfect fulfilling career, etc. . . . Allow yourself to feel all of the wonderful emotions connected to your living this, your highest and greatest good. Relax for a few moments as you contemplate these feelings. . . . Remain completely at peace. . . . Now, silently thank God for this life. . . . Continue to breathe gently, inhale peace and tranquility and exhale all tension. . . . After a few moments, and when you are ready, take another gentle breath, and as you exhale, return to full consciousness, knowing that all you need and desire is waiting for you, and open your eyes.

Highest and Greatest Good Affirmation

I choose to live my highest and greatest good each and every day of my life. I am at peace, living in perfect harmony with all of life. Spirit guides me and cares for me. I am truly blessed. Thank you, God/Goddess/Spirit/Universe, for an unlimited life of joy, abundance, prosperity, good health, and love. And so it is!

Important Points to Remember

- It is your divine right to experience and live your highest and greatest good.

- *We must choose to live our highest and greatest good.*

- If you have a sincere need, the Universe is more than willing to help you fill that need.

- Sacred Signs are one way of relaying that need to God.

- You may communicate with Spirit, your Source, your Creator, at any given moment.

- There is a more valuable lesson that goes beyond your connection to God. It is to express that connection as a vital force in your life, and in the world.

- We must transcend the challenges life presents to us, with a loving and patient heart.

- Live your beliefs and practice them in your daily life.

- The formula for a fulfilling life is dedication to living a sacred life, commitment to personal spiritual growth, and determination to serve God and all life on the Earth.

- Our greatest good comes to us when we accept that it is possible to live a happy and fulfilling life, and not a moment sooner.

- Along with your sacred sign work and other spiritual skills, practice positive spiritual psychology.

- Follow the twenty-two spiritual guidelines to receive and live your highest and greatest good.

Sacred Sign
Journal

SACRED SIGN JOURNAL

Date you asked for the sign _3/5/07 (9 PM)_

Date you received the sign _____

Reasons/intention for asking for the sign
looking for an answer that my future

The specific sign you are asking for (if applicable)
that a man or woman will tell me what a great wife I would make to some man

Your sacred sign statement
within 24 hours I will have a sign that I will meet my future husband in march 2007,

How the sign manifested in your life
_____

Your feelings about the process
excited

Additional comments
I'm lonely, I want someone to come home to, to love, honor & cherish me,

SACRED SIGN JOURNAL

SACRED SIGN JOURNAL

Date you asked for the sign _____

Date you received the sign _____

Reasons/intention for asking for the sign

_____

_____

_____

The specific sign you are asking for (if applicable)

_____

_____

_____

Your sacred sign statement

_____

_____

How the sign manifested in your life

_____

_____

_____

_____

Your feelings about the process

_____

_____

_____

_____

Additional comments

_____

_____

_____

_____

SACRED SIGN JOURNAL

SACRED SIGN JOURNAL

Date you asked for the sign _____

Date you received the sign _____

Reasons/intention for asking for the sign

_____

_____

_____

The specific sign you are asking for (if applicable)

_____

_____

_____

Your sacred sign statement

_____

_____

How the sign manifested in your life

_____

_____

_____

_____

Your feelings about the process

_____

_____

_____

_____

Additional comments

_____

_____

_____

_____

SACRED SIGN JOURNAL

SACRED SIGN JOURNAL

Date you asked for the sign _____

Date you received the sign _____

Reasons/intention for asking for the sign

_____
_____
_____

The specific sign you are asking for (if applicable)

_____
_____
_____

Your sacred sign statement

_____
_____

How the sign manifested in your life

_____
_____
_____
_____

Your feelings about the process

_____
_____
_____
_____

Additional comments

_____
_____
_____
_____

SACRED SIGN JOURNAL

SACRED SIGN JOURNAL

Date you asked for the sign _____

Date you received the sign _____

Reasons/intention for asking for the sign

_____

_____

_____

The specific sign you are asking for (if applicable)

_____

_____

_____

Your sacred sign statement

_____

_____

How the sign manifested in your life

_____

_____

_____

_____

Your feelings about the process

_____

_____

_____

_____

Additional comments

_____

_____

_____

_____

SACRED SIGN JOURNAL

SACRED SIGN JOURNAL

Date you asked for the sign _____

Date you received the sign _____

Reasons/intention for asking for the sign

_____

_____

_____

The specific sign you are asking for (if applicable)

_____

_____

_____

Your sacred sign statement

_____

_____

How the sign manifested in your life

_____

_____

_____

_____

Your feelings about the process

_____

_____

_____

_____

Additional comments

_____

_____

_____

_____

SACRED SIGN JOURNAL

SACRED SIGN JOURNAL

Date you asked for the sign _____

Date you received the sign _____

Reasons/intention for asking for the sign

_____

_____

_____

The specific sign you are asking for (if applicable)

_____

_____

_____

Your sacred sign statement

_____

_____

How the sign manifested in your life

_____

_____

_____

_____

Your feelings about the process

_____

_____

_____

_____

Additional comments

_____

_____

_____

_____

SACRED SIGN JOURNAL

SACRED SIGN JOURNAL

Date you asked for the sign _____

Date you received the sign _____

Reasons/intention for asking for the sign

_____

_____

_____

The specific sign you are asking for (if applicable)

_____

_____

_____

Your sacred sign statement

_____

_____

How the sign manifested in your life

_____

_____

_____

_____

Your feelings about the process

_____

_____

_____

_____

Additional comments

_____

_____

_____

_____

SACRED SIGN JOURNAL

SACRED SIGN JOURNAL

Date you asked for the sign _____

Date you received the sign _____

Reasons/intention for asking for the sign

_____

_____

_____

The specific sign you are asking for (if applicable)

_____

_____

_____

Your sacred sign statement

_____

_____

How the sign manifested in your life

_____

_____

_____

_____

Your feelings about the process

_____

_____

_____

_____

Additional comments

_____

_____

_____

_____

SACRED SIGN JOURNAL

SACRED SIGN JOURNAL

Date you asked for the sign _____

Date you received the sign _____

Reasons/intention for asking for the sign

_____

_____

_____

The specific sign you are asking for (if applicable)

_____

_____

_____

Your sacred sign statement

_____

_____

How the sign manifested in your life

_____

_____

_____

_____

Your feelings about the process

_____

_____

_____

_____

Additional comments

_____

_____

_____

_____

SACRED SIGN JOURNAL

SACRED SIGN JOURNAL

Date you asked for the sign _____

Date you received the sign _____

Reasons/intention for asking for the sign

_____

_____

_____

The specific sign you are asking for (if applicable)

_____

_____

_____

Your sacred sign statement

_____

_____

How the sign manifested in your life

_____

_____

_____

_____

Your feelings about the process

_____

_____

_____

_____

Additional comments

_____

_____

_____

_____

SACRED SIGN JOURNAL

SACRED SIGN JOURNAL

Date you asked for the sign _____

Date you received the sign _____

Reasons/intention for asking for the sign

_____

_____

_____

The specific sign you are asking for (if applicable)

_____

_____

_____

Your sacred sign statement

_____

_____

How the sign manifested in your life

_____

_____

_____

_____

Your feelings about the process

_____

_____

_____

_____

Additional comments

_____

_____

_____

_____

SACRED SIGN JOURNAL

SACRED SIGN JOURNAL

Date you asked for the sign _____

Date you received the sign _____

Reasons/intention for asking for the sign

_____

_____

_____

The specific sign you are asking for (if applicable)

_____

_____

_____

Your sacred sign statement

_____

_____

How the sign manifested in your life

_____

_____

_____

_____

Your feelings about the process

_____

_____

_____

_____

Additional comments

_____

_____

_____

_____

SACRED SIGN JOURNAL

SACRED SIGN JOURNAL

Glossary

Affirmations

Positive statements that inform the Universe/God of what we want to draw into our lives. Affirmations are crucial in attracting what we want because they embody our true intention and the essence of what we need or desire, and so they must be worded carefully. Once an affirmation is released, it works as a magnet to draw our desires to us.

Angel

One of the most powerful loving energies in the Universe, an angel is assigned by God to protect and guide humans, and all other forms of life. They are sacred energies that have never had a physical lifetime. Angels are the guardians of all life, and even guide us through and beyond our death.

Circumstance Signs

Sacred signs that reveal themselves through certain circumstances. A circumstance is defined as a condition or state through which a sign appears. With circumstance signs, certain conditions or surrounding elements contribute to the revelation of the sign. Those conditions that exist surrounding the delivery of a sign are more diffi-cult to understand, and must be interpreted carefully.

Divine Communication Model

A representation of the concept of communication. For communication to exist there must be certain elements present such as a sender, message, receiver, and feed-back. In sacred sign work all must exist and do, therefore, resulting in direct com-munication with the Divine.

Dream Signs

Sacred signs that are revealed through dreams. The Universe may use our dreams to deliver its signs or messages. Some people are more receptive to this sort of medium than others are. The sign is clearly perceived upon awakening. These signs may be easily discernable or require further in-depth interpretation.

Event or Personal Incident Signs

Sacred signs that are revealed through occurrences that happen seemingly unbe-knownst to an individual, and apart from their control. The intuition can perceive whether the event is meaningful or not. Along with the intuition, these signs need the help of logic and reasoning to be interpreted fully.

General Signs

A sacred sign whose method of revelation is left up to the discretion of the Universe. General signs simply ask the Universe for an answer without requesting specific cri-teria for its manifestation.

Go Signs

Sacred signs that encourage the seeker to make decisions, proceed with an action, or notify him or her that their present course of action will glean positive results. They answer "yes/no" questions.

God/Goddess/Spirit/Universe

The Source of all creation—life itself. The perfect energy from which everything in the Universe was created. God is the beginning and the end, the all-good, all-loving energy that pervades the cosmos. It is an immanent, neutral Spirit energy that loves and supports its creations. All life comes from it and returns to it.

Intention

The underlying reason why we do or do not do something. It can be positive, which will yield positive results, or negative, which will result in the opposite. Either way, our true intention determines the outcome of what we attract into our lives.

Keys to the Knowledge of the Universe

The Keys are three mistake-proof ways or steps to discern sacred signs, as well as all other messages we might receive from the Universe. They are specific tools that enable us to communicate on a regular basis with God. The Keys are: Ask, Accept, and Trust.

Master Teacher

Master Teacher is an unseen entity on the astral plane of existence, who is available to us to instruct, lead, or guide. These energies have made profound contributions to humankind and might include such personalities as Jesus Christ, Buddha, and other enlightened souls. Their intervention may be requested when asking for a sacred sign.

Meditation

A silent form of introspection, prayer, and relaxation. Generally, one assumes a comfortable position, closes the eyes, and allows all thoughts to leave the mind while concentrating on a peaceful idea or image, hence achieving an altered state of consciousness.

Mind Signs

Sacred signs that reveal themselves through the seeker him- or herself, as inspired thought or intuition. This sign may be deduced through a series of meaningful occurrences or synchronicities that the seeker has received through the environment or significant circumstances.

Multiple Signs

The manifestation or revelation of more than one sacred sign pertaining to the request and intention of the seeker. There may be occasions when a seeker will ask for one sign and receive several. The Universe tends to send multiple signs when a seeker needs further convincing to take a specific course of action.

Negative Signs

Sacred signs that may be requested or not, and are unwanted because they contradict our specific desires or goals. This type of sign bears a "no" response to a sacred sign request that may be upsetting to the seeker, because it is not the answer he wished to receive. They may also manifest as spontaneous warning signs. Their messages are often ignored or denied.

Ritual

A personal or public spiritual practice performed with regularity to worship, give thanks, or manifest, by recognizing and honoring the existence of a higher power and its assistance in our lives.

Sacred Sign

A revelation from the spirit world, or God/Goddess/Universe, that manifests most often in material form. A sign may be requested by a seeker to assist in decision-making or problem-solving, or may occur spontaneously, without specific request, to inform him or her of an impending situation, or guide them to a possible course of action.

Sacred Sign Process

The ultimate synthesis of the sacred sign method from start to finish, to which a seeker may refer when working with signs. The nine steps clarify and simplify the process and serve as a point of reference for anyone wishing to request sacred signs.

Sacred Sign Statements

Statements that are equivalent to affirmations, constructed by a seeker to request a sacred sign. They consist of a specific request, and a declaration of gratitude to God. These statements must be carefully worded, and are the primary vehicle for sending the seeker's intention to the Universe. They may be general or specific in nature, to reflect a particular time period or form in which the seeker wishes the sign to appear.

Sign Abuse

The extreme form of sacred sign work, in which seekers, encouraged by the appearance of signs in their lives, constantly request them. There is no real danger in this action, but it could lead to potentially dependent behavior in some unbalanced individuals. Such people would use the sign work as a crutch for not taking responsibility for lives or their actions.

Sign Appearance Checklist

Seven guidelines set up to alleviate any confusion, and assist the sign worker in recognizing, understanding, and interpreting his or her sacred sign. This checklist will help the seeker to integrate the message or guidance the sign has delivered into his life.

Specific Signs

A sacred sign whose method of revelation is specifically requested by the seeker. These signs ask the Universe for a specific tangible manifestation, according to the seeker's own criteria. Timing may also be specified.

Spirit Guides

An energy entity existing on the astral plane whose function is to advise, guide, and assist humans in living a positive, abundant, and peaceful life. Spirit guides are energies that have lived in human form and have an agreement with a specific individual, made prior to reincarnation, to remain as a helper in spirit while the individual lives out a physical lifetime. Guides, as they are known, are our best friends in Spirit, helping us get through the day-to-day struggles of life.

Stop Signs

Sacred signs that are clear indicators that the seeker should not be taking an action he or she had planned to take. They are definite "no" responses to a request. These signs require the seeker to trust in the guidance of the Universe, and accept that the advice is given in his or her highest and greatest good.

Synchronicity

A term coined by Carl Jung to describe the meaningful coincidences that occur in our lives. The term implies that the Universe is not random and that all things happen for a reason. Therefore, there really are no coincidences, only meaningful synchronicities, happening just as they are meant to happen, in perfect order, and in their perfect time.

Unexpected or Spontaneous Signs

Sacred signs that are not specifically requested by a seeker. They occur spontaneously without direct invocation, and may manifest to warn, inform, or encourage the seeker. We are often recipients of this type of sign, but do not recognize it as such while it is manifesting. It may be a spontaneous spiritual response to our thoughts and desires at a specific time in our lives.

Warning Signs

Sacred signs that warn the seeker of an upcoming event that may have great impact upon his life. A warning sign might not be easily recognized until the resulting situation has manifested. It may be complicated to interpret, and is easily ignored or denied by a seeker, because it may portend a potentially upsetting or frightening experience.

Bibliography

Belhayes, Iris, with Enid. *Spirit Guides: We Are Not Alone.* San Diego, CA: ACS Publications, Inc., 1985.

Burnham, Sophy. *A Book of Angels: Reflections on Angels Past and Present and True Stories of How They Touch Our Lives.* New York: Ballantine Books, 1990.

Chopra, Deepak. *The Spontaneous Fulfillment of Desire: Harnessing the Infinite Power of Coincidence.* New York: Harmony Books, 2003.

_____. *How to Know God: The Soul's Journey into the Mystery of Mysteries.* New York: Harmony Books, 2000.

Dossey, Larry. *Healing Words: The Power of Prayer and the Practice of Medicine.* San Francisco: HarperSanFrancisco, 1993.

Dyer, Wayne W. *The Power of Intention: Learning to Co-create Your World Your Way.* Carlsbad, CA: Hay House, Inc., 2004.

_____. *10 Secrets for Success and Inner Peace.* Carlsbad, CA: Hay House, Inc., 2001.

_____. *Wisdom of the Ages: 60 Days to Enlightenment.* New York: HarperCollins, 1998.

Hay, Louise L. *Inner Wisdom: Meditations for the Heart and Soul.* Carlsbad, CA: Hay House, Inc., 2000.

Myss, Carolyn. *Sacred Contracts: Awakening Your Divine Potential.* New York: Three Rivers Press, 2003.

Virtue, Doreen. *Earth Angels: A Pocket Guide for Incarnated Angels, Elementals, Starpeople, Walk-Ins, and Wizards.* Carlsbad, CA: Hay House, Inc., 2002.

_____. *Divine Prescriptions: Using Your Sixth Sense—Spiritual Solutions for You and Your Loved Ones.* Los Angeles: Renaissance Press, 2000.

Weiss, Brian, L. *Eliminating Stress, Finding Inner Peace.* Carlsbad, CA: Hay House, Inc., 2003.

Wilde, Stuart. *Infinite Self: 33 Steps to Reclaiming Your Inner Power.* Carlsbad, CA: Hay House, Inc., 1996.

_____. *Sixth Sense: Including the Secrets of the Etheric Subtle Body.* Carlsbad, CA: Hay House, Inc., 2000.

Zukav, Gary, and Linda Francis. *The Heart of the Soul: Emotional Awareness.* New York: Simon and Schuster Source, 2001.

Index

Thanks for reading. To receive my free Positive Talk Newsletter full of helpful, up-lifting, spiritual advice for all phases of life, visit www.AdrianCalabrese.com. While you're there, you may request information about my books, audiocassettes, lectures, and my revolutionary "Tummy Talk: Speak Yourself Slim, Positive Self-Talk Weight Loss System." You may read articles I have written, view my appearance schedule and class offerings, and hear my live five-minute lecture on how to live a joyful and mag-ical life. You may also send an email to me through the web site. Unfortunately, I am unable to do any personal consulting or counseling by email or telephone, but I in-vite you to share your own sacred sign stories with me.

For information about the Metaphysical Center and the Metaphysical Church of the Spirit, visit: www.TheMetaphysicalCenter.org.

May God bless you, and as always,
Go in Light, Love, and Peace. And so it is!